DATE DUE

Demco, Inc. 38-293

Imperial Ends

The Decay, Collapse, and Revival of Empires

Alexander J. Motyl

COLUMBIA UNIVERSITY PRESS   NEW YORK

#45757759

8-16-04

Columbia University Press
Publishers Since 1893
New York, Chichester, West Sussex
Copyright © 2001 Columbia University Press
All rights reserved

Library of Congress Cataloging-in-Publication Data
Motyl, Alexander J.
    Imperial ends : the decay, collapse, and revival of empires / Alexander J. Motyl.
        p. cm.
    Includes bibliographical references and index.
    ISBN 0–231–12110–5 (alk. paper)
        1. Civilization, Western—Philosophy. 2. Civilization, Modern—20th
    century—Philosophy. 3. Europe—History—1871–1918. 4. Soviet Union—
    History—1985–1991. 5. Revolutions. 6. Nationalism—History—20th century.
    7. Turkey—History—Revolution, 1918–1923. I. Title.

    CB245 .M66 2001
    321'.03—dc21

                                                                        2001017098

∞

Casebound editions of Columbia University Press books are printed on permanent
and durable acid-free paper.
Printed in the United States of America

c 10 9 8 7 6 5 4 3 2 1
p 10 9 8 7 6 5 4 3 2 1

To my parents

Contents

She felt like she was slipping endlessly downward.

Monica Vitti, in Michaelangelo Antonioni's *The Red Desert*

Imperial Ends

Introduction: Finding Empire

Empire is back in fashion.[1] Not since the end of European rule in Africa and Asia galvanized social scientists in the aftermath of World War II has there been as much interest among scholars in what S. N. Eisenstadt once called "this very delicate balance."[2] Historians, of course, have had a long-standing interest—going back to at least Edward Gibbon—in particular empires.[3] Archaeologists and anthropologists have investigated a variety of ancient or extinct civilizations.[4] International relations (IR) theorists have written extensively about imperialism.[5] But empire, as a distinctly *political* system, has received scant attention from social scientists; the last four decades of the twentieth century witnessed the appearance of only a handful of books and articles. Until recently, Michael Doyle's truly was a voice in the wilderness.[6]

Several reasons for this lacuna come to mind. One is conceptual. Empires are hard to pin down and define. Scholars generally agree that empires are multinational and politically centralized, but what state is not? Are empires repressive multinational states? Are they very big multinational states? Are they repressive *and* big multinational states? Or are they just great powers?[7] No answer obviously leaps to mind and no answer could—the etymology of *empire* can tell us only how the term has been used and not what the concept means—until we first make a conceptual leap toward it.[8]

Another reason—theoretical—has to do with the hybrid nature of empires. As a polity that is simultaneously an international actor and a peculiarly structured political system with a core and peripheries, empire fits awkwardly in research agendas. IR theorists can easily accommodate empires as great powers but not as systems.[9] Some, such as Yale Ferguson and Richard Mansbach, subsume empires under the category of "polities," thereby transforming them into but one species of a huge genus.[10] Comparativists have an even harder nut to crack, as international relations are traditionally outside their field of interest, whereas hybrid entities with a core and peripheries appear to be both more and less than the systems or states the comparativists usually study.

A third reason may be historical. The last of self-styled empires—those of the British, Dutch, French, and Portuguese—disappeared in the aftermath of World War II. While decolonization generated some interest in empire, it understandably focused attention on such postcolonial tasks of "political development" as participation, penetration, and legitimation, along with the crises and sequences presumably involved.[11] That literature was both enormous and influential, whereas the comparable political science literature on imperial dissolution was tiny. Even now, the recent resurgence of interest in empires pales in comparison to the far greater interest in political development's reincarnation as transitions to democracy, the market, civil society, and rule of law.[12]

A fourth reason may be political. Although mainstream scholars largely ignored empire, those on the Right and on the Left did not. Non-Russian nationalists denounced the Soviet Union as an empire—the histrionics of the Anti-Bolshevik Bloc of Nations were an especially good example of such rhetoric—but their political agendas tainted the concept and led to its becoming identified with "rabid anticommunism" and "cold war messianism" in the liberal—that is to say, in the mainstream scholarly—mind.[13] President Ronald Reagan's characterization of the Soviet Union as an "evil empire" merely confirmed these suspicions. Together with the concept of totalitarianism, which also suffered from guilt by association, empire became a litmus test of political attitudes in general and of attitudes toward socialism and capitalism in particular.[14]

The Left also contributed to politicizing the concept of empire by applying it only to the United States and its often aggressive, exploitative, and imperialist behavior abroad. Left-wing critics were absolutely right to criticize U.S. imperialism but dead wrong to define empire and imperialism only in terms of capitalism. This conflation of definitions and causation— traceable at least to J. A. Hobson, Rudolf Hilferding, and V. I. Lenin—meant that capitalism, and only capitalism, produced imperialism and that, in turn, imperialism was merely its highest stage.[15] This maneuver reduced the

USSR to a simple multinational state and excluded precapitalist empires from analysis or exposed them as being "really" capitalist. Another unfortunate consequence of the Left's conceptual sloppiness is that, with the demise of the USSR and its universal rechristening as an empire, the left-wing critique of the United States appears both irrelevant and quaint today.

These excellent reasons for ignoring empires notwithstanding, we cannot. Important as historical reality, conceptual category, and analytical device, empires refuse to go away. Fortunately, we need not fret excessively about the obstacles to grasping them. Defining empires may be difficult, but it cannot be impossible. Theorizing about empires may be a challenge, but it is not insurmountable. History can neither set agendas nor undermine them. And politics, while unavoidably embedded in everything scholars do and say, should no more trouble us than the air, however polluted, that we breathe.

Empire Redux

The sudden unraveling of the USSR was the puzzle that revived the interest in empires. The abrupt and peaceful end of a superpower manifestly had something to do with the Soviet Union's internal constitution. And yet, although multinationality, hypercentralization, and other features frequently associated with empire had long been evident to Soviet nationality experts, if not to mainstream Sovietologists, they were rarely conceptualized in imperial terms.[16] Hélène Carrère d'Encausse's provocative study of Soviet decline sparked a minor storm in 1979 because it dared to suggest that the "nationality question" was the Soviet Union's Achilles' heel and that empire was an appropriate scholarly designation for such a polity.[17]

It took the intervention of non-Russian popular fronts, which began referring to the USSR as an empire during the years of perestroika, to purge the term of its pejorative connotations.[18] Once that happened, empire became politically respectable. And once the Berlin Wall fell and the USSR collapsed, cold war agendas appeared either moot or even persuasive. The conjunction was perfect: something exceptionally dramatic had happened to an entity that one could, without fear of violating academic norms of semantic rectitude, call an empire.

Ironically, the Soviet Union "became" an empire at the very moment it ceased to exist.[19] As Mark Beissinger notes, calling the USSR an empire has become as de rigeur at present as shunning the label used to be in the past.[20]

Such terminological ups and downs are of interest—especially in what they have to say about the sociology of the group using the terms—but they should not distract us from, or be confused with, the actual concepts and their empirical referents. Communities of people do not become nations simply because we wish to imagine them as such; regimes do not become democratic just because we use the modifier; and political entities do not become—or stop being—empires merely because terminological fashion says so. Concepts usefully apply to reality if and only if we can isolate their defining characteristics *and* find appropriate empirical referents. Far more than wild-eyed imagination and inventive whim is involved.[21]

Concepts

The concepts that are central to this book, both substantively and organizationally, are empire, decay, attrition, collapse, and revival. Others, such as continuity, formality, decline, and disassemblage, will also rear their heads but as spin-offs of these five.

- I define *empire* as a hierarchically organized political system with a hublike structure—a rimless wheel—within which a core elite and state dominate peripheral elites and societies by serving as intermediaries for their significant interactions and by channeling resource flows from the periphery to the core and back to the periphery.
- Continuous empires are tightly massed and, in all likelihood, territorially contiguous; discontinuous empires are loosely arranged and often involve overseas territories.
- The core elite's rule of the periphery may be formal, involving substantial meddling in the personnel and policies of the periphery, or informal, involving significantly less interference and control.
- Decay is the weakening of the core's rule of the periphery.
- Decline is a reduction in the imperial state's power in general and military capability in particular.
- Disassemblage entails the emergence of significant interperiphery relations and spells the end of empire as a peculiarly structured political system.

- Attrition is the progressive loss of bits and pieces of peripheral territories.
- Collapse is the rapid and comprehensive breakdown of the hublike imperial structure.
- Revival, or reimperialization, is the reemergence of empire—that is to say, the reconstitution of a hublike structure between a former core and all or some of the former periphery.

As with all concepts, no clear-cut, nonsemantic line divides continuity and discontinuity, informality and formality, and so on.[22]

Despite the length of its subtitle, this book explicitly aims *not* to provide the last word on all aspects of empires but only to make sense of the downward slope of their trajectories. My approach is structural, less so because I am wedded to its charms and rather more so because the alternative—agency oriented, choice centered, and intentionalist—persuades me even less. Because incompleteness and imperfection distinguish theory from faith, structural theories, like all theories, are severely flawed. The structural framework I use in this book is also flawed, and I make no attempt to hide its wrinkles, cracks, and scars. Quite the contrary, I shall push the theory as far as it can go while purposely exposing its weaknesses and showing at which points it, like some stubborn mule, can be budged no further and when, exhausted by its own weight, it just falls to the ground. This exercise in self-reflective theorizing may or may not persuade readers, but at least they will or will not be persuaded for the right reasons.

I start the story in the middle, with an analysis of empires as peculiarly structured political systems. I ask why such systems are prone to decay, why some decayed empires experience attrition and others do not, why some collapse by falling apart rapidly and comprehensively, and why some collapsed empires—including, perhaps, the former Soviet empire—then revive. I argue that the very structure of empires promotes decay and that decay in turn facilitates the progressive loss of territory. At any point of this trajectory, shocks can intervene and lead to collapse. Throughout the book I claim to have isolated, at best, the necessary and facilitating—*not* sufficient—conditions of the phenomena I explore. I borrow shamelessly—especially from historians, whose understanding of individual empires is infinitely more sophisticated than mine—and make no claims for earth-shattering originality.

Although I am fully aware of the impossibility of divorcing normative concerns from the social sciences, I do wish to emphasize that, my use of

declinist terminology notwithstanding, I do not necessarily share the pessi-
mism of, say, an Oswald Spengler.[23] The "good" society, whether imperial
or not, need not be doomed to decline because of what makes it good. By
the same token, I see no reason to share the optimism of a Francis Fukuyama
and conclude that the good society must triumph because of what makes it
good.[24] A declinist teleology is the flip side of a belief in progress.[25] Although
these beliefs cannot, as beliefs, be refuted or confirmed, the experience of
the twentieth century—human rights, democracy, and international institutions on the one hand, and world wars, genocides, and totalitarian systems
on the other—may provide some grounds for being skeptical of both.[26]

Debts

This book is dreadfully old-fashioned. It draws its primary inspiration—
not from recent theoretical developments in IR, comparative politics, and
other branches of political science—but from a collection of half-forgotten
articles written many years ago. I have several reasons for bucking fashion.
First, the political science literature has, as I have already noted, relatively
little to say about empires. Second, many of the more recent contributions
strike me as riddled with fatal failings. Foremost among them is a penchant
for "theories of everything"—explanatory frameworks that attempt to account
for more, indeed much more, than they, or any theory, possibly can—and
for theories that privilege agency, choice, and intention.[27] Third, the IR
literature that anthropomorphizes "the state"—which is to say, the IR literature—thereby engages in the crudest form of reification and, by using predicates of the form "the state does," lapses into semantic meaninglessness.
There is, I fear, little to be learned from theories that operate on such pre-
carious assumptions.[28] Last but not least, I am genuinely impressed by the
contributions of three scholars.

Conceptually, I am indebted to Johan Galtung, whose "structural theory
of imperialism" underpins my definition of empire and, more generally, my
preferential option for a structural approach to empire. Although Galtung's
theory is not without flaws—for one thing, it is not really a theory—it remains
a model of clear thinking that, to my mind at least, has gotten empire just
about right.[29]

Theoretically, I draw on Karl Deutsch's theory of "disintegration in totalitarian systems."[30] Deutsch's remarkably prescient analysis is, I shall argue,

of equal relevance to empires, not because empires are totalitarian but because Deutsch's theory is structural and because the structures of empires and totalitarian states are isomorphic. Structural isomorphism means that a structural theory of totalitarian disintegration is, ipso facto, a structural theory of imperial decay.

Empirically, I cannot overstate the importance to this enterprise of Rein Taagepera's painstaking plotting of the rise, persistence, and fall of virtually all historical empires.[31] In a series of articles written over two decades, Taagepera calculated and plotted the areas over time of more than one hundred empires and great powers. Although Taagepera's primary concern was to explain variation in the height (territorial expanse) and length (temporal existence) of empires, I submit that his central contribution is that he demonstrated that all imperial trajectories are fundamentally alike and that the ideal trajectory resembles a parabola.[32] As mine is primarily a work of interpretation, the vast amounts of information contained in Taagepera's parabolas serve as this study's de facto empirical foundations. My discussion of individual empires is thus purely illustrative of the empirical trends that Taagepera identified.

Because imperial trajectories have a definite geometric shape, Taagepera's parabolas permit me to claim that parabolas may be considered the geometric equivalent of algorithmically compressible data and thus as close to "lawlike" as is possible in the social sciences.[33] In turn, Galtung and Deutsch permit me to argue that imperial decay is a consequence of the intrinsic features of empires as peculiar kinds of structured systems. With parabolic trajectories driven by decay as the norm, it follows that nonattrition and collapse must be anomalies and thus the products of intervening or exogenous variables.

To argue that the life span of all empires would, *other things being equal*, resemble a parabola is to engage in a counterfactual. As I shall make frequent use of counterfactual conditionals in this book, it is important to understand what counterfactuals do and do not entail in general and for my project in particular. James Fearon has argued that comparativists must resort to counterfactuals in order to enlarge the number of cases underpinning their otherwise empirically impoverished theories.[34] In other words, counterfactuals supposedly help corroborate a theory. But that, alas, is exactly wrong. Counterfactual conditionals cannot and do not corroborate some theory, T, because, as Nelson Goodman has shown, counterfactuals presuppose laws — or, in the case of the social sciences, theories. We are entitled to engage in "what if" scenarios, not because they provide additional evidence of the validity or invalidity of T but because a different theory, T', permits us to consider what would have happened if some premise were different from the reality.[35]

Use of the ceteris paribus clause is therefore premised on some existing theory—namely, T'—that claims to have isolated a causal relationship between two or more factors. Imagining other things as being equal presupposes an underlying theoretical connection. In this sense, the clause clears the air and lets us see further and better. My argument thus rests on an implicit use of ceteris paribus. I claim that Taagepera's parabolic plotting of the rise and fall of empires *would* be the norm for all empires, if other factors did not intervene. Such an argument can be persuasive if and only if lawlike empirical evidence exists to support it—and, I submit, Taagepera's parabolas provide that evidence because they establish a uniformity for a large N, and a conceptually coherent explanatory story—that is to say, a theory, in this case Deutsch's—underpins it. To be sure, where some see uniformity, others may see variation. Imperial trajectories may *really* resemble parabolas, as I claim, or the parabolas may be the exception to a rule that resembles a crazy zigzag. Both approaches are a priori legitimate, although the social scientific preference for regularities and patterns would, for reasons that postmodernists would probably reject, favor the former.

Overview

Chapter 1 examines the concept of empire and defines it as a political system characterized, as Galtung noted many years ago, by a peculiar kind of structure. The relations of dominance between the core elite and the peripheral elites have a hublike structure: that is, peripheries interact with one another politically and economically via the core. In this sense, and in this sense only, empires are structurally isomorphic with totalitarian states. I continue with a general discussion of political systems, of systems theorizing, and of what structural theories can and cannot do. I conclude with a critique of commonly encountered claims—all agency oriented, choice centered, and intentionalist—about empire and of theories of everything. If such approaches and their instantiation, rational choice theory, are as useless as I believe them to be, structural approaches to empire can only be less bad. Chapter 2 begins with a discussion of Taagepera's parabolas, arguing, as I have already noted, that they represent an algorithm for a large N of empires. Proceeding from the structural isomorphism between empires and totalitarian states and drawing on Deutsch's structural explanation of totalitarian disintegration, I then argue that imperial structure holds the key to the secular tendency of core-periphery relations to loosen and thus to decay. More important, I argue that Deutsch effectively provides the theoretical underpinnings of the algorithmic regularity expressed in the downward slope of Taagepera's parabolas. As such, Deutsch's theory amounts to something like a "covering law" of imperial decline.[36] Chapter 2 also discusses how attrition takes place, by means of war and liberation struggles, and why.

Chapter 3 first examines one exception to this rule—the nonattrition of obviously decayed empires—and explains this anomaly in terms of intervening variables, those indispensable theoretical devices that invariably pull social science from the brink of predictive failure and, in our case, "prop up" the imperial structure and keep it whole.[37] Chapter 3 then examines another exception to this rule—imperial collapse. I suggest that system-shattering events that no theory of empire can predict or explain push imperial systems over the edge. The best one can do is suggest which kinds of shocks are likely to affect which kinds of empires under which kinds of conditions.

Chapter 4 looks at the aftermath of collapse and suggests that reconstitution is for the most part a function of four structural variables: the extent of decay, the evenness of decay, the relative power of the former core, and the continuity of the former empire. One combination precludes imperial revival, as in the case of the Habsburg and Ottoman Empires after 1918. Another promotes revival, as in post-Romanov Russia. A third may, as with interwar Germany, lead to attempted revival.[38] I then transpose these arguments to the post-Soviet context. The east-central European polities appear to have escaped post-Soviet Russia's sphere of influence completely, whereas the non-Russian republics are still precariously positioned between independence, hegemony, and empire. For better or for worse, the case for "creeping reimperialization" culminating in partial revival is not unpersuasive. Several exogenous factors will promote that process. The expansion of the North Atlantic Treaty Organization (NATO) and the European Union (EU) on the one hand and globalization on the other will isolate Russia and its neighbors, thereby promoting their dependence on one another and facilitating the institutional repenetration of the periphery by the former core.

Finally, the conclusion briefly examines the implications of Russian imperial revival. Post-Soviet Russia's structural resemblance to a decaying empire may ultimately doom any imperial project and perhaps Russia itself. Although reimperialization is only possible, the collapse of a revived Russian empire is probable, and instability, insecurity, and conflict in the formerly Soviet space are virtually certain for some time to come. Evidently, structural theories may not be without policy relevance.

In Lieu of a Preface

Besides relegitimizing the study of empire, the Soviet Union's collapse also precipitated my interest in empires. After all, if the USSR fell apart because it was an empire, a closer look at empires, both historically and theoretically, promised a better understanding of the Soviet case. Astute readers will have no difficulty seeing that my thinking about the Soviet Union has influenced my thinking about empires as much, if not more than, the reverse.

My thinking about empires is, like this book, the product of much zigging and zagging. I had written a number of papers, some published, some unpublished, on empire in the mid-1980s and 1990s and felt emboldened in late 1996 finally to write a book.[39] It soon became obvious that, while the papers were more or less consistent with one another, many of the arguments were not. Smoothing out the rough edges and eliminating the contradictions has been an enlightening exercise, partly for what I have relearned about the complexity of empires and mostly for what I have come to understand about the exceedingly tricky business called theorizing.

I have been struck yet again by the overdetermination of facts and the underdetermination of theory and by the concept-dependence of both.[40] For better or for worse, we live in a theoretically plural world, and to deny that fact, as the professional dynamics of the social science profession compel us to do, cannot be good for scholarship, policy making, or personal integrity. Nor, on the other hand, can it be good to follow the fashion that confuses conceptual chaos with conceptual pluralism. Concepts provide us with excellent means of negotiating treacherous theoretical waters. Because the concepts used by a theory must be coherent and fit one another, fuzzy concepts, like weak foundations, cannot sustain even the most richly empirical and theoretically flamboyant edifices. The proposition is hardly new, having been advocated by Giovanni Sartori for many years, but, alas, it needs repeating.[41]

Readers should not be surprised that, despite its use of such words as *algorithm, lawlike,* and *counterfactual conditional,* this book neither tests a theory nor proves that others fail tests. Except for conceptual incoherence, there is, I suspect, no test that a minimally coherent theory can fail so completely as to be discredited.[42] Whatever the reason for the social science profession's declared infatuation with positivist procedure, I do not share it. And, as the remarkable capacity of good, bad, and god-awful theories to survive all manner of assaults and even achieve hegemony suggests, neither does the profession.[43]

A large number of colleagues have provided criticism, comments, and guidance in the course of this project. They are, I am certain, fully responsible for the parts of this book that make most sense. Many thanks go to Dominique Arel, John A. Armstrong, Karen Ballentine, Karen Barkey, Mark Beissinger, Mark Blyth, Ian Bremmer, Michael Brown, Rogers Brubaker, Yitzhak Brudny, Walter Clemens, Alexander Cooley, Istvan Deak, Oded Eran, Valentina Fedotova, Stephen Handelman, Leonid Heretz, Ersin Kalaycıoğlu, Juozas Kazlas, Paul Kolstoe, Viktoriya Koroteyeva, Taras Kuzio, David Laitin, Allen Lynch, Michael Mandelbaum, Warren Mason, Rajan Menon, Gusztav Molnar, Andrew Nathan, Laszlo Nemenyi, Barnett Rubin, Zoltan Rostas, Nikolai Rudensky, Nadia Schadlow, Oleh Shamshur, Corinna Snyder, Jack Snyder, Ronald Grigor Suny, Raphael Vago, Mark von Hagen, and Veljko Vujacic. Special thanks also go to Seweryn Bialer, Irwin Selnick, Richard Rudolph, David Good, and the late William McCagg, who first got me thinking about the USSR as comparable to Austria-Hungary and other empires.

To the Smith Richardson Foundation goes an especially large dollop of gratitude for providing me with the funding to take a leave of absence in the fall of 1998. Without its generous support, this book, like so many empires, might have taken an inordinately long time to end.

1 Imperial Beginnings

Because Johan Galtung's structural theory of imperialism is central to my thinking on empire, starting our discussion of imperial systems with a closer look at his contribution will be useful. "Briefly stated," writes Galtung, "imperialism is a system that splits up collectivities and relates some of the parts to each other in relations of harmony of interests, and other parts in relations of disharmony of interests, or conflict of interests."[1] Galtung then unpacks this definition:

> Imperialism is a relation between a Center and a Periphery nation so that 1) there is harmony of interest between the center in the Center nation and the center in the Periphery nation [where, as Galtung notes, the center is "defined as the 'government' (in the wide sense, not the 'cabinet')"], 2) there is more disharmony of interest within the Periphery nation than within the Center nations, 3) there is disharmony of interest between the periphery in the Center nation and the periphery in the Periphery nation.[2]

Several features of Galtung's definition strike me as inadequate. First, I prefer to call this set of relationships *empire*: imperialism is a policy, whereas political relationships constitute a polity. Second, to define the center as the *government* is too restrictive for the core—a variety of political and economic elites are usually implicated in empire—and plain wrong for the periphery, as the concept of government suggests that the periphery possesses sovereignty. And, third, Galtung's use of the term *nation* is either incorrect, if it refers to country or state, or almost primordial in its implications, if it refers to a culturally delimited group or community of people.

These conceptual criticisms notwithstanding, Galtung has made a critically important—and mercifully pithy—contribution to our understanding of empire. First, he has underlined that empire is about relationships. Second, he appreciates that empire necessarily presupposes a distinct center in the "Periphery nation": "where there is no bridgehead for the Center nation in the center of the Periphery nation, there cannot be any imperialism by this definition."[3] In other words, what I call the core elite must have a partner in the periphery, or what I term a *peripheral elite*. Third, Galtung understands that empire benefits both centers (or elites, in my terminology); empire is not—indeed, it cannot be—a one-way, zero-sum relationship. Fourth, Galtung's scheme permits empire to arise in any number of ways—via outright aggression or quietly, even surreptitiously.[4] And, fifth, although Galtung does suggest that imperialism is possible in a "two-nation world"—a possibility that I shall decisively reject—he also notes that, within imperial relations, "interaction between Center and Periphery is vertical," whereas "interaction between Periphery and Periphery is missing."[5] As will presently be clear, all these points are also found, if in translation, in the analysis that follows.

Hubs and Spokes

I start with the commonsense proposition that an empire minimally involves a non-native state's domination of a native society. Both parts are housed in territorially distinct regions inhabited by culturally distinct populations—the non-natives and the natives—who share physically real or merely imagined characteristics and are different, with respect to these characteristics, from other populations in other regions.[6] The region housing the non-native state may be termed the core (or metropole), whereas the native regions are the periphery, or, more exactly, peripheries.[7] D. W. Meinig usefully breaks down what he calls the center and the periphery into subcategories: capitals (the seats of authority), cores (the areas immediately adjacent to the capitals and populated by the non-natives), and domains (the areas surrounding the cores and less densely populated by the non-natives).[8] The distinctions are important, but the binary opposition between core and periphery and non-natives and natives will suffice for our purposes (in addition to, perhaps, eliciting nods of approval from postcolonial theorists).

A few examples will convey the plausibility of this starting point.

- The Assyrian Empire was centered in the cities of Ashur, Nineveh, and Calah in northern Mesopotamia, whereas imperial territories extended from the Mediterranean to the Persian Gulf.
- The Achemenid Empire had Persia as its core, with Pasargadae and Persepolis serving as capitals, and a periphery consisting, after Darius's administrative reorganization, of twenty provinces ruled by satraps.
- The Roman Empire was centered in Italia, whereas its far-flung territories ringed the Mediterranean.
- The core of the Ottoman Empire—like that of Byzantium—was Constantinople and its hinterland was in Rumelia and Anatolia (as was Byzantium's); peripheral Ottoman territories were scattered throughout the Balkans, the Near East, the Arabian Peninsula, and northern Africa.
- The historically Habsburg crown lands, with Vienna as their center, served as the culturally German core of the empire, whereas the other territories were the non-German periphery.
- St. Petersburg and Moscow constituted the core of the Russian Empire, whereas the provinces extending in a vast arc from Finland through Ukraine, Transcaucasia, and Turkestan to the Far East were the periphery.
- European Russia in general, and the area spanning the Moscow-Leningrad axis in particular, served as the core of the Soviet empire, housing the central apparatus of the totalitarian state and the Russian or Russified core elite. The Soviet periphery consisted of three sets of entities: the non-Russian regions of the Russian Soviet Federated Socialist Republic, the fourteen non-Russian Soviet Socialist Republics, and the people's democracies of east-central Europe.
- The distinction between core and periphery was most obvious in the French, British, Spanish, Dutch, German, and Portuguese Empires, all of which possessed a core in their nation-state and peripheries for the most part overseas.

We expect core elites to run the agencies, organizations, and institutions of the imperial state, and we expect peripheral elites to administer their peripheral counterparts or extensions. The Roman Empire provides a good example of this division of labor. "Roman practice was to rule through the intermediacy of the governing bodies of settled and formally constituted communities," writes Gary B. Miles. "The responsibilities of local leaders . . . provided them with occasions both to exercise power and extend patronage, through the collection of taxes, administration of justice (and thus keeping of the peace), recruitment of soldiers, and organization of corvées when Rome required local roads, postal service, or the like."[9] These "power elites," to use C. Wright Mills's felicitous phrase, are not and need not be monolithic or, as John Armstrong demonstrates, even ethnically homogeneous.[10] The Ottoman core elite, for example, consisted of the sultan and his family; the "divans or councils that deliberated on affairs of state; the *kadı* courts; the imperial hierarchy of religious colleges; the Janissary infantry corps"; and the "ruling class," consisting of the "men of the sword," "men of religion," palace service, and "men of the pen."[11] In Han China the men of the pen, or literati, were an especially important component of the elite in both core and periphery.[12] In the Soviet Union the core elite consisted of those members of the nomenklatura who occupied positions of authority—in the Communist Party, government, army, and secret police—in Moscow and its environs.[13]

Core elites craft foreign and defense policy, control the armed forces, regulate the economy, process information, maintain law and order, extract resources, pass legislation, and oversee borders. In turn, peripheral elites implement core policies. In a word, the division of labor between core elite and peripheral elites in empires is little different from that between central elite and regional elites in all states. Although the relationship between core elite and peripheral elites is unequal, premised as it is on the dominance of the former and the subordination of the latter, that too is no different from center-periphery relations in many multinational dictatorial or, more generally, hierarchically organized states.

Constructing Empire

How are we to cross the boundary between nonempire and empire? I propose moving beyond the functional division of labor between core elite and peripheral elites and examining their relationship in terms of the imperial whole and all its parts. Bruce Parrott defines empire as "a dominant society's control of the effective sovereignty of two or more subordinate societies that are substantially concentrated in particular regions or homelands within the empire."[14] We can now see why there must be at least two peripheries. As long as the core elite has only one peripheral unit to dominate, we can never transcend the functional division of labor and establish a definitional boundary for empires. But once there are at least two such units, it becomes possible to relate the parts of an empire to the systemic whole, as in figure 1.1, and actually to speak of a defining structure.

Core-periphery relations in an empire resemble an incomplete wheel, with a hub and spokes but no rim. The most striking aspect of such a structure is not the hub and spokes, which we expect to find in just about every political system, but the absence of a rim—or, to use less metaphorical language, of political and economic relations between and among the peripheral units or between and among them and nonimperial polities (designated as Z in figure 1.1). Galtung also speaks of the "interaction structure" of empires as being vertical between center and periphery and as missing between periphery and periphery.[15] Communist Czechoslovakia could not by this logic have been an empire, because the Czech regions dominated only Slovakia; Tito's Yugoslavia was not an empire because the national republics enjoyed significant relations with one another and with the outside world. In contrast, the Spanish Empire in the Americas was quintessentially im-

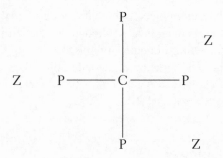

Note: C = core; P = peripheries, Z = nonimperial polities.

FIGURE 1.1 The Structure of Empire

perial in structure: all the provinces possessed direct political and economic links to Spain but not to one another. As Gerhard Masur points out, "American goods en route from one side of America to the other had to travel circuitously through Spanish ports, and Spanish navigation had a monopoly on trade with the colonies."[16] Similarly, Meinig suggests that the late eighteenth-century British Empire should be envisioned as "two great sectors of concentric patterns, a radiating set of provinces—anchored on a single point—ringing much of the North Atlantic."[17]

Inasmuch as everything is connected to everything else, it is physically impossible to keep the peripheries of even the most hierarchically organized empire completely separate or isolated. If nothing else, smuggling, everyday human contacts, and chance encounters are inevitable. By the absence of a rim, therefore, I must mean that no significant relations between peripheries and between peripheries and other polities can exist without the intermediation of the core. Significance is anything but a straightforward notion, of course, especially as we approach the conceptual middle between what is obviously significant and obviously insignificant.[18] Even so, the notion of significance entitles us to expect that, in an empire, political consultations, military cooperation, and security arrangements between peripheries take place only, or largely, on the initiative and under the leadership of the core. By the same token, most exchanges of resources—money, goods, information, and personnel—will also take place via the core. Note that the kind, or mix, of resources that flow in an empire can be defined only relationally, in terms of the imperial economy.[19] Ancient empires are likely to have seen flows of material goods; modern empires would have witnessed shifts toward financial flows. In particular, as Arnold Toynbee notes, "Communications . . . are the master-institution on which a universal state [i.e., empire] depends for its very existence. They are the instruments not only of military command over its dominions, but also of political control."[20]

The transportation networks of empires (roads, railroads, sea links, pipelines, and the like), which are the physical channels through which resources flow, generally reflect this hublike structure. In the overseas empires of the British, French, Germans, Dutch, and Portuguese, natural resources were transported from the hinterlands to the coasts of colonies, where they were loaded onto ships that brought them to Europe, which then supplied the colonies with manufactured goods. A more complicated arrangement might involve triangular relationships, such as the transatlantic slave trade, whereby manufactured goods went from England to Africa, which supplied slaves to the American colonies, which in turn shipped raw materials to England. Many centuries earlier, goods, people, and finance traveled along roads and sea routes to and from such imperial capitals as Rome and Constantinople. Romanov Russia's railroad system had St. Petersburg and Moscow as its hub. In Austria-Hungary roads, railroads, and telegraphs centered on Vienna and to a lesser degree on Budapest and Prague—as we would expect in a severely decayed empire. The Soviet transportation network had Moscow as its reference point, so that even in the late 1980s it was most convenient to travel between republics via the Soviet capital. The Inca system of roads was not, strictly speaking, organized around a hub—the Incan Empire was squeezed between the Pacific Ocean and the Andes—but the capital city, Cuzco, was the center to which all roads led.[21]

Significantly, empires, as I have defined them, bear structural resemblance to totalitarian states.[22] Both types of polities consist of central and peripheral entities implicated in a relationship of dominance, control, and supervision by the former of the latter. In empires these entities are geographically delimited—the core versus the territorial periphery; in totalitarian states they are functionally delimited—the core state versus core and peripheral societies, economies, and cultures. Obviously, totalitarian states are infinitely more totalizing than empires, but the two do have an identical hublike structure: a conceptually distinct core that dominates conceptually distinct peripheries bound minimally to one another. As we shall see in chapter 2, we can draw important theoretical lessons from this isomorphism.

Types

Although all imperial polities possess certain defining characteristics— above all, structure—that enable us to subsume them under a single political genus regardless of the time, place, or circumstances in which they existed, empires are sufficiently diverse to warrant dividing them according to types. As the defining characteristic of greatest relevance to us is structure, it makes sense to make structural variation the key to an imperial typology. One obvious structural feature is the length of the spokes. Some empires are territorially concentrated, whereas others, consisting of far-flung, even overseas, possessions, are not. That is, the imperial wheel can be small, with short spokes, or large, with long ones; more likely than not the wheel will not be circular because it will have both long and short spokes.

A second, equally obvious, feature is the number of spokes—that is, of core-periphery relationships. That number can range anywhere from two to N, where N is some number less than the total number of potential peripheries in the world at any time. I term empires with few, short spokes *continuous* and those with many, long spokes *discontinuous* (see figure 1.2). In general, continental, or territorially contiguous, empires tend to be continuous (although very large continental empires obviously will not be), whereas overseas, or maritime, empires are almost invariably discontinuous. Empires may also be both continuous and discontinuous, or *hybrid*, thus resembling a "noncircular" wheel. The Habsburg Empire was highly continuous, the British Empire was discontinuous, and the German Reich, with imperial possessions in Europe, the Pacific, and Africa, was a combination.

A variety of scholars also differentiate empires according to the extent of authority, or rule, exerted by core elites over peripheral elites. As David Lake suggests, peripheral elites with least authority are said to participate in a formal empire; those elites with more substantial amounts—the USSR's east-central European satellites, for instance—belong in an informal empire.[23] Table 1.1 details these and related distinctions. In formally ruled empires the core elite appoints and dismisses the peripheral elites, sets the entire internal policy agenda, and determines all internal policies. In an informally ruled empire the core elite influences the appointment and dismissal of peripheral elites, sets the external policy agenda, influences the internal agenda, and determines external policies while only influencing internal

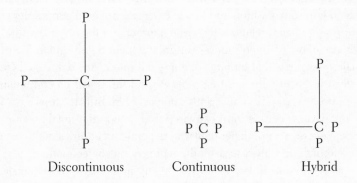

FIGURE 1.2 Types of Empires

TABLE 1.1 Types of Core Rule

	Hegemonic	Informal	Formal
Peripheral elite		(Appointed/dismissed)	Appointed/dismissed
Policy agenda	External	External/(internal)	[No external]/internal
Policies	(External)	External/(internal)	[No external]/internal

Note: Parentheses designate a weak form of control over the action within the empire; brackets designate the absence of that activity.

policies. In a hegemonic nonimperial relationship, such as that between the United States and many Latin American countries, the dominant polity has little or no voice regarding the appointment and dismissal of elites and internal agendas and policies.[24] At most, it determines the external policy agenda and influences external policies.

Although the formal/informal distinction is relevant to understanding imperial trajectories, strictly speaking it is not a feature of empires, as are continuity and discontinuity, but of rule, whether imperial or not. The rule of some imperial peripheries may be formal and of others informal, but all regional elites in all states are also subject to greater or lesser degrees of central control. In nondemocratic states, for instance, rule is much more formal than in democratic states. The formal/informal distinction therefore says far less about empire per se than does structure: although subordinate to the core in some fashion and to some degree, imperial peripheries enjoy few or no significant relations with one another and the outside world.

My use of binary oppositions—continuity/discontinuity and formality/informality—suggests that empires perforce fall into neatly delineated either/ or categories. Naturally, most empires at most times will be combinations of the extremes as well as of various midtypes. The British Empire is a case in point, having been, as John Darwin puts it, "a constitutional hotch-potch of independent, semi-independent and dependent countries, held together not by formal allegiance to a mother-country but by economic, strategic, political or cultural links that varied greatly in strength and character."[25] Reality may be messy, but that is all the more reason to use concepts that are less so.

Systems

Conceptualizing empires as hublike arrangements between a core and its peripheries amounts to saying that empires are, as S. N. Eisenstadt recognized many years ago, *political systems*.[26] Empires consist of distinct units—the core state and elite and the peripheral elites and societies—that are constituent parts of a bounded and coherent imperial whole. These units occupy specific places within the empire; their characteristics are defined relationally; and the relations between core and periphery are structured in a way that defines the system as a whole. Empires are thus structurally centralized political systems within which core elites dominate peripheral societies, serve as intermediaries for their significant interactions, and channel resource flows from the periphery to the core and back to the periphery.[27] Metropoles that command peripheries to interact significantly would in essence be withdrawing from empire. Empire ends, then, not when or because the core ceases to dominate the peripheries but when or because the peripheries implicated in such domination begin to interact with one another significantly. Thus the *P-C-P* relationship can be as tight or as loose as possible, but empire will exist as long as *P-P-P* or *Z-P-Z* relationships are weak or insignificant or nonexistent. (Hence my preference for the term *disassemblage* to the simpler, more elegant, but less accurate *dissolution*.)

As systems, empires are bounded sets of interrelated, interactive, and interdependent parts.[28] Systems can be biological, ecological, cultural, linguistic, social, economic, political, and so on.[29] Ponds, rain forests, tribes, languages, markets, and polities can all have systemic characteristics, and they can all behave as systems without being identical.[30] Immanuel Wallerstein and James Rosenau even conceptualize the world as a system. Wallerstein focuses on the core and the periphery of a capitalist world system, whereas Rosenau includes states, collectivities, nongovernmental organizations, firms, and even individuals in his systemic model.[31]

To make the claim that empires, like other entities, may be usefully conceptualized as systems is not to endorse every aspect of the systems theorizing and/or structural functionalism associated with Talcott Parsons, Niklas Luhmann, Claude Lévi-Strauss, or David Easton.[32] To be sure, one cannot make just any claim about systems. The view of empires as systems does oblige us to regard systemic functioning, or stability (Rosenau speaks of "order"), as a given and to distinguish between the "inside" and the "outside" of the system.[33] It may also, as I shall suggest shortly, compel us to transfer some causal sources of systemic change to the outside, the environment. Each move has potentially troublesome implications, but none is fatal—or, to put it more accurately, no more fatal than moves that flow from other conceptualizations.

The criticism that systems theorizing takes stability as its baseline and treats change as the puzzle is thus fully justified.[34] Where the criticism is entirely off the mark is in suggesting that systems theorizing is therefore either wrong or anomalous. All theories take certain things for granted and, in so doing, convert other things into puzzles. Rational choice theory, for instance, assumes rationality and puzzles over irrationality. "Irrational choice theory," which would be perfectly possible to construct, would do exactly the opposite.[35] One could, by the same token, just as easily start with change and puzzle over stability. There may be excellent normative or practical reasons for doing so but no purely theoretical ones.

The distinction between inside and outside, meanwhile, is no less common to nonsystemic approaches. Every theory, every analysis, every set of concepts has its own specific social science domain. No theory, no analysis, no set of concepts can, or should, address everything (and to the extent that Wallerstein and Rosenau do, they may be rightfully criticized for attempting to construct a theory of everything). In that sense, what is outside the domain is outside the system of thought as well. By the same token, although every theory hopes to account for every cause of some effect as well as for every effect of some cause, as a theory rooted in concepts rooted in language it perforce cannot attain either goal. Nolens volens, some causes and effects will always be outside the theory.

Stability

Because our baseline is systemic stability, an ideally functioning imperial system should, logically and obviously, persist indefinitely. Because empires resemble giant machines consisting of interlocking, interdependent parts arranged in, to use Eisenstadt's phrase, a "very delicate balance," they should hum along so long as the parts fit and function. It is reassuring to know that the expectation of longevity is not unwarranted. Many empires do have remarkable staying power. The Romans maintained imperial rule for about five centuries, the Byzantines for almost 1,000 years, the Ottomans for more than 500, and the Habsburgs and Russians for more than 400. The Persian, Mongol, French, British, and Dutch Empires performed less impressively, surviving about two centuries apiece, and the Soviets managed to stay in power for only 80 years. Nevertheless, Eisenstadt was surely right to observe that empires have "provided the most massive and enduring form of government man had known prior to the modern period."[36]

Fully cognizant of the perils posed by theories of everything, I suggest that the hublike structure of empire can provide for stability—and therefore promote persistence—on at least two levels.

First, empire is an effective mechanism for channeling resources and providing security. The P-C-P channel permits investment, goods, and people to move around a complex system coordinated by core elites and institutions. Empires resemble federal systems in having the capacity to transfer resources from richer regions to poorer ones and for connecting faraway provinces to metropoles.[37] Relatedly, continuous empires are excellent mechanisms for promoting the common defense—assuming, again, that the elites are not, or not yet, rapacious and exploitative. Just as the core can accumulate and distribute economic resources via imperial channels, so too can it mobilize and deploy the armed forces and military resources needed to defend a large realm. In particular, the core of a continuous empire can effectively counter threats by using internal lines of communication. As Edward Luttwak has argued, the Roman Empire, as a discontinuous realm surrounding a large body of water, lacked this advantage and had to deploy troops permanently along its frontiers.[38]

Second, the hublike structure promotes both the core elite's dominance and its acceptance by the peripheral elites. The core elite is, by definition, more resource rich and powerful than any one peripheral elite. Other things being equal, peripheral elites can challenge the dominance of the core elite only if two or more of them band together. Empire addresses this threat in simple structural terms. First, that peripheral elites (ideally) interact via the core means that their capacity to communicate and thus to band together against the core elite is limited. In particular, no one peripheral elite can halt the flow of resources and information from the periphery to the core and back. Second, because all peripheries are simultaneously contributors and recipients of resources, peripheral elites are, structurally, competitors and not cooperators. Their dependence on the core, and their resulting independence of each other, aligns them with the core and against the rest of the periphery. Third, empires are extraordinarily good deals for peripheral elites. Although the images of empire conjured up by Frantz Fanon and other nationalists suggest that peripheral elites are oppressed and humiliated, we know from Galtung that the structure of empire actually promotes their elite status by guaranteeing their continued governance of peripheral baili-wicks.[39]

Miles shows how these factors contributed to the absence of "nationalist rebellions" against Roman imperial rule. Thus "this reliance on local aris-tocracies . . . united to Rome the interests of those who already held positions of power and influence among the native populations."[40] Moreover, the absence of horizontal, interperiphery means of communication meant that "traditional leaders . . . might indeed bring the common cause they shared with other communities or other tribes to the attention of their followers, but the very structure of the political situation would mean that individuals participated in common undertakings as members of separate and distinct followings. . . . Ancient alliances, therefore, were characterized by a partic-ular precariousness."[41]

Change

If systems are presumed to be stable, how and why should they ever undergo change? Like all social science puzzles, this particular puzzle is puzzling at first glance only. There is, after all, no reason for us not to locate potential sources of change both outside and inside the system. Exogenously generated change would involve shocks, an indispensable concept I return to later. Endogenously generated change would have to be consistent with the system itself. But how can endogenously generated change both derive from the system *and* be consistent with its bias for stability? We can square this circle, thanks to structure.

Let us look at the inside of a system more closely. Robert Jervis claims that, because change in any one part of a system necessarily affects all other parts, and because other things can therefore never be held constant, in principle it is impossible to claim, in straightforward social scientific fashion, that A causes B.[42] But if linear cause-and-effect relationships are absent from systems, systems analysis is of little use to social scientists with just such concerns on their minds. Jervis therefore concedes that certain relations are more obviously central than others — if only because some change could not possibly affect all elements of a system equally.[43] It is these more salient relationships that give a system the property of structure. (As Luhmann notes, systems "could not exist without structure."[44]) But with structural relations in place, we can posit causes and effects, which in turn provide us with a mechanism for accounting for change. Stability may still characterize systems as systems, but their central property—structure—can now serve as a source of change.

Easton suggests that structures may be theorized as limiting the range of systemic tendencies, producing specific outcomes, or facilitating certain tendencies.[45] The first effect is easiest to imagine. If a system has a certain structure, it cannot, ipso facto, have another and will not be susceptible to its influence. As a result, structures may be said to narrow the range of systemic outcomes. System A will not and cannot experience any form of "B-ness," just as system B will not and cannot experience any form of "A-ness"—except as one of the myriad unintended and unpredictable consequences that rightly concern Jervis. This seems to be a trivial conclusion but only at first glance. It is not, I suggest, wholly uninteresting to know that structures narrow the range of the possible.[46]

The second consequence strikes me as being most difficult to entertain. Even if it were conceivable for structures to generate specific systemic outcomes, it is hard to see how, given the relative nonlinearity built into systems, we could ascertain that particular results were determined by structures only and not by other factors as well. More fundamentally, I do not see how structures, as systemic properties, could produce specific outcomes. A structural fault may cause a building to tilt, thereby increasing its chances of, but not directly causing, collapse. An organizational structure may increase efficiency and morale, but it cannot cause complete efficiency and happiness. By the same token, Kenneth Waltz suggests that bipolar international systems tend to be more stable—where stability is defined as the absence of war—than multipolar ones, regardless of whether their constituent parts, the states, are more or less stable.[47] The property of tallness can, by analogy, promote certain behaviors, such as basketball playing, and discourage others, such as being a jockey, and it may be both a necessary and facilitating condition of being a basketball star, but it cannot serve as a sufficient condition of such an outcome. In promoting certain tendencies, therefore, structures can have a probabilistic effect on concrete outcomes but not a determinative causal one.

The third effect is thus of greatest importance. Some systemic tendencies will be likely, or more likely, to occur because the kind of relationships characterizing a system's units may facilitate just these, and not other, tendencies. Where relationships are complementary, systems will "work." Where relationships are not complementary, and perhaps are even contradictory, systems will "not work." Some such dynamic concerns Janet L. Abu-Lughod as well: "In a system, it is the *connections* between the parts that must be studied. When these strengthen and reticulate, the system may be said to 'rise'; when they fray, the system declines."[48] In particular, some systems will thrive and do well because their structure promotes the efficient use of resources. Other systems will run down and do poorly because their structure promotes the inefficient use of resources. As long-term tendencies and not immediate effects, both "working" and "not working" are compatible with our starting point, systemic stability.

Karl Marx's explanation of capitalist decline is an excellent illustration of "not working." The ideal version of capitalism he constructs necessarily has a tendency to run down, as the rate of profit declines in the long run. But, while withering away is inevitable, systemic collapse becomes very probable, "in the final analysis," happening only for extratheoretical reasons. Indeed, Marx is forced to rely on metaphors to make the point: "Centralisation of the means of production and socialization of labour at last reach a point where they become incompatible with their capitalist integument. This integument is burst asunder. The knell of capitalist private property sounds. The expropriators are expropriated."[49] In contrast, Barrington Moore's explanation of the "social origins of dictatorship and democracy," while Marxist in inspiration, succeeds at establishing that social structures matter to the emergence of different types of regimes but fails to show that they necessarily led to certain outcomes and not to others.[50]

Equally illustrative is Plato's discussion of the decay of the just city. *Justice* refers to the relations between and among the various categories of people inhabiting the republic: it consists in their doing only what they do best and in not trespassing onto others' domains. Because they do not sustain this structure of relations, decay sets in: "Those whom you have educated to be leaders in your city, though they are wise, still will not, as their reasoning is involved with sense perception, achieve the right production and nonproduction of your race. This will escape them, and they will at some time bring children to birth when they should not."[51] The accident of bad birth subverts the compartmentalization at the core of the republic. "As a result you will have rulers who do not have the proper guardians' character to test the races of Hesiod and your own—the golden, silver, copper, and iron races. Iron will then be mixed with silver and copper with gold, and a lack of homogeneity will arise in the city, and discordant differences, and whenever these things happen they breed war and hostility."[52] The city then degenerates, inexorably moving through timocracy, oligarchy, and democracy and ending with dictatorship.

Structure

Structural theories of system breakdown have, as Mark Hagopian has pointed out, a certain structure.[53] First, they identify a structural contradiction, that is to say, an incompatibility between the relations within which the units of a system are enmeshed. For Marx, a true structuralist, the contradiction is between the relations of production and the mode of production; for Chalmers Johnson, the disequilibrium is the result of systemic decay on the one hand and elite intransigence regarding reform on the other; for Theda Skocpol, the contradiction is between the imperatives of international anarchy, which results in competition and war, and the class-derived limitations on state autonomy; for Joseph Tainter, the tension is between systemic complexity and systemic efficiency; for Frantz Fanon, the contradiction is between the native's humanity and the colonizer's inhumanity.[54] In each case, and in sundry others, the structural contradiction weakens the existing system and ultimately wears it down. Capitalist societies suffer from growing immiseration and a declining rate of profit; prerevolutionary societies become increasingly disequilibrated or insufficiently modernized; complex societies become inefficient; colonial societies develop deep antagonisms between rulers and ruled.

Second, such theories then posit a trigger, accelerator, spark, or shock that pushes rotting systems over the edge.[55] Because structures promote only tendencies, logically no reason exists that contradictions should not, on their own, lead only to the continued withering away of the systems involved and thus only to the heightened probability of certain outcomes. Dramatic caesurae, such as revolutions, breakdowns, and collapses, therefore require that something happen to make sudden ruptures in an otherwise smooth process possible. For Marx, the "capitalist integument" bursts; for Johnson, accelerators intervene; for Skocpol, weak states lose wars; for Tainter, "stress surges" happen; for Fanon, the "guns go off by themselves."[56] Robert Kann's explanation of Austria-Hungary's collapse fits this mold exactly:

The answer to the question of which special circumstances and conditions made the disintegration of the Habsburg monarchy acute is
simple: The World War situation. . . . There exists no adequate evidence that Austria-Hungary, in spite of the imperfect integration of her
peoples and her far less than perfect administrative amalgamation was
bound to break asunder barring the pressure of external events. There
is, on the contrary, good reason to assume that, according to a kind of
pragmatic law of historic inertia, a power complex which had existed
for so many centuries might have continued to exist for some time to
come had it not encountered the forces of external pressure.[57]

Similarly, Cho-yun Hsu notes that Han China's exchange network "was
delicately balanced and could be upset by disturbances such as war or natural calamity, which could break down the national network into several
regional networks."[58]

To be sure, "an external calamity cannot," as Carlo Cipolla insists, "always
be assumed as a sufficient cause of the decline of a civilization." He is also
correct to note that, "more often than not, the question is complicated by
the lack of an adequate response to the challenge, and the lack of response
must be explained."[59] But it is no less important not to assume that the
existence of bona fide shocks is tantamount to the lack of an adequate response. Powerful shocks can destroy just about anything, whereas weak ones
can destroy only weak or weakened objects, but in both cases the shock and
the condition of the affected object are analytically, and empirically, different things.

Structural contradictions therefore require the intervention of outside
shocks for general tendencies to result in particular outcomes. It would be
convenient if contradictions invariably generated, bred, or facilitated corre-
sponding shocks, but we have to recognize that, theoretically and logically,
this need not be the case.[60] We cannot ignore what Herbert Kaufman terms
the "role of chance," or what Machiavelli called *fortuna*.[61] We may prefer
closed theoretical systems to open-ended ones, but no reason exists that
social science theory should not accept, perhaps even embrace, theoretically
exogenous causal factors. Indeed, to acknowledge the importance of exogenous factors is another way of saying that theories of everything are impossible and that some degree of unpredictability is, as James Fearon argues,
unavoidable.[62] Charles Doran goes even further, stating that "forecasts ultimately fail because no technique has been developed that allows the fore-

caster to predict, prior to the event itself, when a nonlinearity ['a total break from the past trend, a discontinuity'] will occur."[63]

No less important, shocks are part and parcel of the everyday explanatory apparatus of the natural and social sciences. The course of evolution, as Stephen Jay Gould reminds us, may be due less to some immanent logic and more to accidents of nature.[64] According to George Soros, emerging markets are supposed to be especially susceptible to financial shocks utterly beyond their control.[65] William McNeill has shown how plagues, and more generally illnesses, have undermined societies.[66] Although the devastation wreaked upon Amerindian societies by European bacteria must, as Cipolla might argue, also be seen in terms of the immunological isolation and hygienic conditions of these societies, certainly the decimation of, say, the Aztecs was overwhelmingly the result of infectious intrusions over which Aztec society had absolutely no control. Brian Fagan extends this argument to "climatic anomalies."[67]

Things obviously get trickier with heroes in history. On the one hand, even extraordinary men and women are the products of their societies, and their ascent to positions of power and influence cannot be divorced from the overall context. And yet we would be hard-pressed to deny that world historical personalities, although products of their times, also have an extra-systemic effect on the very societies that spawned them. Napoleon Bonaparte and Adolf Hitler obviously come to mind. Sidney Hook's discussion of V. I. Lenin is also instructive. According to Hook,

> Without Nicolai [*sic*] Lenin the work of the Bolshevik Party from April to October 1917 is unthinkable. Anyone who familiarizes himself with its internal history will discover that objectives, policy, slogans, controlling strategy, day-by-day tactics were laid down by Lenin. Sometimes he counseled in the same painstaking way that a tutor coaches a spirited but bewildered pupil; sometimes he commanded like an impatient drill sergeant barking at a raw recruit. But from first to last it was Lenin. Without him there would have been no October Revolution.[68]

Hook may or may not have proved his case, but that it is plausible and that Lenin was somehow critical, and surely not incidental, to the revolution is clearly true. Indeed, Alexander Rabinowitch's painstakingly detailed examination of Lenin's decisive role at a crucial central committee meeting just before the seizure of power in November lends Hook's case strong support.[69]

In like fashion, Robert Wesson identifies a "single and all-powerful ruler, whose person is elevated far above ordinary mortals," as the central defining characteristic of empire.[70] Unlike Hook's heroes, however, Wesson's rulers can more easily be translated into mere holders of institutional power—they are, after all, subordinate to the "basic axiom of empire, the dominion of those who are on top, the rule of power for the sake of power"—and thus be reconciled with structure.[71] Even so, no one would dispute that structural accounts of empire do not sit well with emperors in general and charismatic emperors in particular.

Extraordinary circumstances and ordinary structures approximate a crude eclecticism only if the former openly contradict the premises of the latter. While resorting to extrasystemic factors is a blow to theoretical parsimony, it need not be fatal so long as those factors are not incompatible with the conceptual underpinnings of a theory.[72] Only genuine heroes in history, who necessarily make momentous choices, are incompatible with such a theory. Plagues, hurricanes, droughts, and their social equivalents—invasions, wars, economic collapses, and so on—are not. As I argue in chapter 3, a structural theory of imperial decline is least incompatible with structurally—or, at least, unintentionally—generated shocks to the system. That way, both the dynamics of the system and the immediate cause of its breakdown are beyond human choice and thus within the same semantic field.

Maxima Culpa

Besides being intrinsically incapable of accounting for the timing of particular events, structural theories are also open to other accusations. One is that such arguments deemphasize or ignore human behavior. While true enough, this charge misses the point. First, all theories that are not theories of everything deemphasize or ignore something, because all theories can hope to explain only what they purport to be able to explain.[73] Second, although one may insist, à la Anthony Giddens, on the equal theoretical importance of human beings, who presumably complement methodological holism with methodological individualism and structure with agency, such a self-consciously eclectic move either rests on incompatible assumptions (and therefore self-destructs) or amounts to a trivial ontological claim about the reality of people.[74]

There is no alternative to abandoning the quest for theories of everything and choosing—between contradictory and thus incompatible premises in general and between structure and agency in particular.[75] Either alternative is perfectly legitimate, because both structure and agency can on their own generate coherent theoretical accounts. "Methodologically socialist" approaches are, as Arthur Danto has shown, no less true than methodologically individualist ones. If, according to Danto, structural statements can be translated into, and therefore reduced to, individualist ones, the latter can also be translated into the former. And if structural statements cannot be translated downward, neither can individualist ones be translated upward. In sum, we have no obvious grounds for claiming that one approach is more basic than, and therefore preferable to, the other.[76] They simply are different. Thus, unless one is wedded to individual choice for nontheoretical reasons, no reason exists for not treating choice as an intermediate step—or a constant form of foreground noise—that does nothing to alter the causal effect of structure on systems.[77] Ironically, as Gabriel Almond points out, rational choice theory does just that. By taking preferences as given and transforming choices into logically necessary behavior, rational choice theory effectively eliminates any meaningful notion of choice from its domain.[78]

Equally misplaced is the charge that structural approaches neglect ideology and culture, issues with which Jack Goldstone, Theda Skocpol, and their detractors, such as Nikki Keddie and Said Amir Arjomand, have grappled.[79] There is little to say in response to this accusation, except to admit that it is justified. By the same token, we would, in the spirit of Danto's remarks, also be justified in pointing out that just as structural arguments tend to ignore—and cannot be translated into—ideology and culture, ideological and cultural arguments do not translate into structure. Both approaches are different ways of slicing reality, which is to say that both approaches involve theories that, like all theories, engage in crass oversimplifications.

Structural theories are woefully incomplete theories. But so are all theories. Structural theories neither tell the "whole story"—after all, their function is not to tell the whole story, and telling the whole story is an impossible task anyway—nor provide lawlike explanations of the parts of the story that they do address. Like nets, structural theories catch some of reality and let most of it pass through. And like nets, they catch more and less than they would like to catch. But so do all theories.

Pitfalls

I began this chapter by placing the cart before the horse. I treated empires as systems partly because they can usefully be conceptualized as such, and partly because my approach to explaining imperial trajectories is structural, and structures presuppose systems. But I have opted for a structural theory of empire not because structural approaches are the best—that they certainly are not—but because they are the least bad. Their flaws strike me as far less egregious than those of their leading competitor—agency-oriented, choice-based, intentionalist accounts. Indeed, structural carts help us steer clear of pitfalls commonly encountered in studies of empire:

1. *Conflating imperialism with empire*

Imperialism is a policy, whereas empire is a polity, and although it should be obvious that policies and polities are different things, it is remarkable how many scholars—including, alas, Johan Galtung—fail to recognize this elementary point.[80] More important, although policies frequently *are* chosen, polities generally are not.[81] To quote Yale Ferguson and Richard Mansbach: "Some polities prosper, while others wither or nest. In the clashes, both 'winners' and 'losers' are modified and typically assume some of the other's characteristics. Shaped by their own contests as well as broader economic and social trends, polities are always 'becoming.'"[82] And, although the central purpose of expansion may be empire, it is surely untrue that, as Imanuel Geiss claims, the "central purpose of empire is expansion."[83]

2. *Attributing empire formation only to imperialism*

There is no reason that, logically, relations of dominance must be the product only of military expansion purposely intended to create empire. Reinhold Niebuhr puts it well: "The word 'imperialism' to the modern mind connotes aggressive expansion. The connotation remains correct in the sense that empire, in its inclusive sense, is the fruit of the impingement of strength upon weakness. But the power need not be expressed in military terms. It may be simply the power of a superior organization or culture."[84] Empire comes into being anytime its defining characteristics are clustered in some time and space.[85] Imperial relations may therefore emerge quietly, as the result of subtle shifts over time in power, wealth, and status. The historical record offers many examples of dynastic unions between powerful and weak monarchs that led to the incorporation of the latter's realm on imperial terms. "Ready-made" peripheries can be bought or otherwise acquired, perhaps by thievery, guile, or stealth.[86] Geir Lundestad even speaks of "empire by invitation."[87] And, as Geoffrey Parker notes, it is "anachronistic . . . to see the West as bent upon world domination from the voyage of Vasco da Gama onwards. In fact, the Europeans originally came to Asia to trade, not to conquer."[88]

3. *Interpreting empire formation and imperial decline as the product of choice*

Although it may be true that leaders of state can desire empire, it makes little sense to claim that they "choose" empire or any of its subsequent trajectories, such as persistence, decay, or collapse. In the vast majority of cases of empire formation, no logically or empirically identifiable point exists at which such a choice could be contemplated and, least of all, made. Elites could choose to buy or steal or marry into ready-made empires—precisely those instances of empire formation that choice-centered accounts usually ignore—but they surely do not choose empire when and if they choose to attack a state. Choosing to attack may be to choose imperialism, but, unless we conflate empire with imperialism, that too is not to choose empire. Even if we grant that elites can choose empire, it strains the imagination to think that they would choose collapse, which is tantamount to collective suicide, or could choose persistence or decay. As the latter usually takes place over hundreds of years, during which time millions of choices are made, it would be as unhelpful to suggest that any one choice was decisive as it would be useless to claim that millions of choices mean that choice matters. Finally, even if choice matters, it is obviously true that—pace the language and logic of much IR theory—"states," as clusters of institutions, cannot possibly choose. To claim otherwise is to lapse into reification and anthropomorphism of the worst kind.[89]

4. *Explaining empire formation and imperial decline as the product of conscious cost-benefit analysis*

We have no reason to suppose that imperial elites are capable of measuring or even appreciating the "real" costs and benefits of empire.[90] Elites may be blinded by myths, ideologies, and strategic cultures (of which more later); more important, measuring the costs and benefits of empire may be impossible except in some rough and painfully obvious way—when, for instance, continual humiliating defeats on the field of battle obviously suggest that something is wrong. How, exactly, are contemporaries—or, for that matter, scholars—supposed to say whether the acquisition or loss of some territory, big or small, was a cost or a benefit or both?[91] What time line is significant? Whose standards of cost and benefit are we to use? Whose costs are real costs, and whose benefits are real benefits? (Analogously, whose interest is the "national interest"?) If elites benefit from a territorial acquisition, is that good or bad for the empire? What if the masses benefit? The multiplicity of questions suggests that using a cost-benefit analysis, by anyone and at any time, may be a chimerical effort. Not surprisingly, D. K. Fieldhouse's study of "economics and empire" strongly suggests that the link between the two was not, as a cost-benefit analysis would require, strong but "coincidental and indirect."[92]

5. *Attributing elite inability to appreciate the "real" costs and benefits of empire to the myths, ideologies, or strategic cultures the elite at one time created in order to advance imperialist agendas*

These myths, accordingly, acquire explosive force and the elites are hoist with their own petard. But why should this happen? Elites do not create beliefs ex nihilo. They have to counter, mold, or refashion existing values, beliefs, and norms. If they can do so at time t, why not at time $t + n$, when experience and maturity should make them all the more capable of effecting ideational change? To state that myths and culture assume a life of their own and become impervious to elite attempts to change them is not to solve the problem but merely to restate it.[93] This is not to say that ideas cannot drive expansion. The Inca belief that dead emperors should inherit the lands they ruled when still alive may, as Geoffrey Conrad and Arthur Demarest suggest, have impelled their successors to seek territory for themselves.[94] But such an argument is utterly unlike the claim that consciously constructed imperialist myths promote imperialism.

6. *Using the concept of overextension or overreach to suggest that empires, like states in general, have an ideal size that should or does guide the policy choices of the elite*

What the optimal size of states could be is, I submit, a mystery.[95] Historically, as today, states have ranged in size, and in resources, population, and the like, from very small to very large. If the world can accommodate Bhutan, Estonia, and Brunei on the one hand as well as the United States, China, and Russia on the other, surely it strains the imagination to think that some size is best. The argument is even weaker in any particular case. Would China be optimal with or without Tibet? With or without Macao?

Would the United States be worse off or better off with or without Rhode Island or Staten Island or even California? Would Canada benefit from Quebec's secession? Did the Czech Republic suffer from Slovakia's departure? To be sure, a certain size — "large" as opposed to "small" — might be optimal for economies of scale; a smaller size might reduce transaction costs; a very small size might, as Jean Jacques Rousseau believed, foster a spirit of togetherness.[96] But is it possible for all these sizes, and a multitude of others, ever to overlap? Surely not. Even if they could at time t, one would have to espouse an unusually static view of life to expect them to remain identical at time $t + n$. And if it is impossible to determine the optimal size of states, it is just as impossible to say that any one state is or is not too large or too small at any particular time.[97]

Choosing Everything

These six pitfalls are, I suggest, the product, either directly or indirectly, of agency-oriented, choice-centered, intentionalist accounts of imperial trajectories on the one hand and of the temptation to create theories of everything on the other. Such accounts are of little use in understanding empire for two reasons. The first is that empires are, as macro units of analysis, on a different level of the ladder of abstraction than such equally abstract micro units as intentions and choices. The second reason goes deeper, addressing the rootedness of agency-oriented, choice-centered, intentionalist accounts in rational choice theory (RCT). As I hinted at earlier, RCT self-destructs upon closer examination.[98] The fatal flaw is the way it deals with human rationality, defined as the maximization of utility, the minimization of risk, or some variant thereof (where both utility and risk are defined in terms of preferences). Given this assumption, RCT can follow one of two equally self-defeating paths. If RCT insists that all human preferences at all times and in all places are identical — say, material — it is making a patently false and easily falsifiable claim. Counterexamples are simply far too numerous. False assumptions matter, because they permit theories to prove anything and thus to parade as theories of everything. If instead RCT accepts diversity of preferences as its axiomatic starting point, it can account for the emergence of preferences only in terms of culture, ideology, institutions, and the like. To do so, however, is to give explanatory priority not to choice — after all, there is nothing to choose — but to culture, ideology, institutions, and so on.

Worse, to accept the diversity of preferences and preference structures necessitates that RCT also admit the a priori possibility of many maximizing and minimizing strategies. Once such a move is made, however, RCT has in effect been reduced to culture, ideology, and institutions. But if culture, ideology, and institutions are "what really matters," RCT is not a theory, but at best a formula, for calculating the effects of culture, ideology, and institutions on human behavior and at worst a random collection of values and operations. Either way, agency disappears from the picture. But if agency is irrelevant to RCT, so too are the agents and their choices. Seen in this light, RCT amounts to a crude form of determinism at best and mystification at worst.

Why then—if this analysis is even minimally persuasive—is RCT virtually hegemonic in the social sciences? One part of the answer must entail the profession's general lack of interest in methodological questions and conceptual issues relating to what makes theories tick. Another part probably involves RCT's ability to generate formulae and use numbers, evidence of its supposedly scientific *and* value-free status. A third may have something to do with the culture that has spawned RCT. It is, one suspects, no accident that notions of rationality and utility maximization have caught on most, if not quite solely, in a country that claims to venerate just these values.[99] Ironically, this third point is most consistent with RCT's own means of accounting for preferences, as described at the beginning of this section.

Rational choice theory is, of course, a theory of everything par excellence, and that failing would be fatal even if RCT were not internally flawed. The problem, as I have already noted, is that theories of everything are not theories. If our goal is theory, and not cosmic faith, we have to recognize that all theories are limited—after all, all theories presuppose initial conditions that limit their range—and thus that a theory of imperial decline cannot account for empire formation and that a theory of empire formation cannot account for imperial decline.[100] Even if decline and formation are mirror images of each other, we have no reason to suppose that one theory could explain a process and its reverse. Just because factors A, B, and C may have been relevant to the emergence of empire does not mean that the absence of A, B, and C must therefore account for the disappearance of empire. If, say, strong metropoles, weak peripheries, transnational forces, and a favorable international environment promote empires, it does not follow that weak metropoles, strong peripheries, the absence of transnational forces, and an unfavorable international environment promote the dissolution of empires. Indeed, any theory claiming to explain both X and *not-X* is probably an exercise in circularity.

Second, theories of X and *not-X*, even if seemingly alike, are different because their initial conditions are miles apart. The central initial condition of empire formation is the nonexistence of empire; that of imperial decline is the existence of empire. Third, because these qualifications apply with equal force to persistence, Taagepera's parabolas reflect at least three distinct and equally complicated theoretical tasks.[101] Finally, the ways in which empires rise and decline are so many and varied—in 1423, for instance, Byzantium sold Thessalonika to the Venetians for 50,000 ducats—that it strains an already overstrained imagination to think that even one complete and unassailable theory of only emergence, of only decline, or of only persistence is possible.[102]

Faute de Mieux

Because agency-oriented, choice-centered, intentionalist accounts are, at best, of limited utility and at worst either self-contradictory or meaningless, the only theoretical alternative is, for better or for worse, structural, not centered on choice, and nonintentionalist. While hardly ideal, such an alternative deals with empire on the requisite level of abstraction and it eschews determinism. Fortunately, structuralist-inspired scholarship is old hat, and its practitioners are many. Consider but three. In *The Structures of Everyday Life* Fernand Braudel focuses on the development of economic forces and material life. In *The Great Wave* David Hackett Fischer examines the rise and fall of prices and their influence on political change. In *Guns, Germs, and Steel* Jared Diamond investigates the effect of environmental factors on the course of human history. All three scholars create compelling narratives that feature no heroes in history.[103]

Closer to home is Michael Doyle's *Empires*. In isolating the factors that promote empires—a strong metropole, a weak periphery, transnational forces, and a favorable international context—Doyle has in effect preferred a structural theory.[104] Thus empires emerge under the following conditions:

> The interaction of a metropole and a periphery joined together by transnational forces generates differences in political power which permit the metropole to control the periphery. This relationship is pro-

duced and shaped by the three necessary features [a "metropole," a "transnational extension of the economy, society, or culture of the metropole," and a "periphery"], which are together sufficient. It is influenced and shaped by the structure of the international system ["which may be unipolar, bipolar, or multipolar"].[105]

Like Braudel's, Hackett Fischer's, and Diamond's, Doyle's account eschews reference to agency, choice, and intention.

One need not fully agree with Doyle's list to appreciate the importance of the claim that empires tend to emerge, persist, or decline when the structural conditions promoting their emergence, persistence, or decline are in place. Although Doyle errs in claiming to have isolated a set of conditions that account for emergence, persistence, *and* decline, his error does have the salutary effect of reminding us that structure is as fallible as agency and that, like agency, it too can underpin theories of everything.

2   Imperial Decay

Empires persist for long, but they do end. Scholars generally agree on what happens. Vigorous and powerful realms progressively become ossified and weak: bureaucracies grow, spending booms, economies falter, battles are lost, rebellions succeed. Most scholars also agree on why breakdown occurs: empires become inefficient and, over time, cease to "work." Not surprisingly, although the following passages are purposely drawn from different contexts and historical periods, they still manage to tell a coherent story that corresponds to the conventional wisdom:

> Throughout history, keeping administrative field officials loyal and obedient to central authorities has been one of the persistent problems of government. Field officers have always exhibited a strong tendency to act independently . . . carv[ing] out little empires for themselves in many places. And although such developments did not necessarily impede the mobilization of resources and the coordination needed to maintain systemwide defenses and construct regionwide public works . . . they tended to make such concerted action more difficult.[1]

> More and more supervision and regimentation by the central bureaucracy was required to keep the administrative machine in motion. The bureaucracy was expanded in number, its quality inevitably sank, and it became increasingly difficult to control its abuses. . . . The expanded bureaucracy, though ill paid, involved a heavy charge in salaries—or,

rather, rations and uniforms; and because it was ill paid and diluted in quality and difficult to control, it was inefficient, corrupt, and extortionate.[2]

In his pamphlet on the *Death of the Persecutors*, Lactantius charges Diocletian with having quadrupled the armed forces and vastly expanded the civil service to the point that soon, as he concludes, "there will be more governors than governed." Bureaucrats swarmed in the late Byzantine Empire, and as Bernard Lewis writes, an "inflated bureaucracy" plagued the economy of the late Arab Empire. About 1740, Macañaz ranked the excessive number of civil servants first in his enumeration of the causes of the decline of Spain. . . . Complaints of this kind are commonly heard in mature Empires.

One of the remarkably common features of empires at the later stage of their development is the growing amount of wealth pumped by the State from the economy. In the later Roman Empire taxation reached such heights that land was abandoned. . . . In sixteenth-century Spain the revenue from the two taxes . . . increased from 1504 to 1596 by more than five times. . . . Figures relating to tax revenues, however, do not always tell the whole story. In the later Roman Empire, in the late Byzantine Empire, in seventeenth-century Spain, inflation was rampant. Debasing the currency is just another form of taxation.[3]

[The Han exchange network] was delicately balanced and could be upset by disturbances such as war or natural calamity, which could break down the national network into several regional networks. Further breakdown could then occur, disintegrating a previously integrated system into a group of communities sustained by local self-sufficiency. The exchange network therefore was rather fragile to serve as the bond holding China together for prolonged periods, vulnerable as it was to foreign invasions, civil wars, and natural calamities.[4]

My story of imperial decay is little different from this one. I have no reason to disagree with the description of decline or with most of the reasons adduced for it. But my account differs from others in the two respects noted at the end of chapter 1. First, I claim to be able to explain not the entire parabolic trajectory but only its downward slope. Second, I root decay in imperial structure and not choice. I thereby avoid the false promise of theories of everything and the false leads of agency-oriented, choice-centered, intentionalist accounts.

Taagepera's Parabolas

Rein Taagepera's great achievement is to have demonstrated that imperial trajectories resemble parabolas of various heights and slopes.[5] The Arab Caliphate (figure 2.1) required about one hundred years to reach its maximum size, around 700 A.D., and then disintegrated during the next two centuries. Similarly, the Mongols (figure 2.2) expanded enormously from about 1200 to 1300 and then, almost immediately thereafter, went into decline, fading away by about 1400. The Ming dynasty (figure 2.3) grew as rapidly, but far less spatially, from the middle of the fourteenth to the middle of the fifteenth centuries and then declined during the next two hundred years. It took the

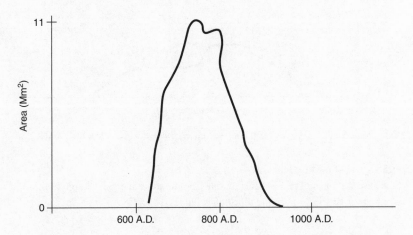

Note: 1 megameter = 1,000 km; 1 sq. megameter (Mm²) = 390,000 sq. miles.

FIGURE 2.1 The Arab Parabola.
Source: Rein Taagepera, "Expansion and Contraction Patterns of Large Polities: Context for Russia," *International Studies Quarterly* 41 (1997): 482.

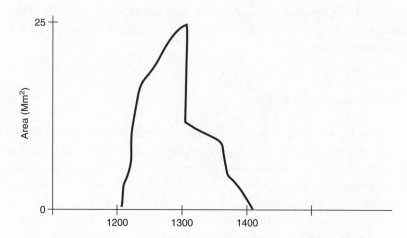

Note: 1 megameter = 1,000 km; 1 sq. megameter (Mm²) = 390,000 sq. miles.

FIGURE 2.2 The Mongol Parabola.
Source: Rein Taagepera, "Expansion and Contraction Patterns of Large Polities: Context for Russia," *International Studies Quarterly* 41 (1997): 483.

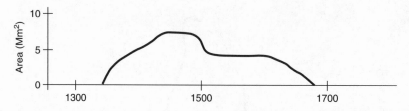

Note: 1 megameter = 1,000 km; 1 sq. megameter (Mm²) = 390,000 sq. miles.

FIGURE 2.3 The Ming Parabola.
Source: Rein Taagepera, "Expansion and Contraction Patterns of Large Polities: Context for Russia," *International Studies Quarterly* 41 (1997): 483–84.

Ottomans (figure 2.4) about two hundred years, from the mid-fourteenth through the mid-sixteenth centuries, to reach the height of their power; they then remained at the top of the parabola for about three hundred years, before losing most of their possessions in the nineteenth and twentieth cen-

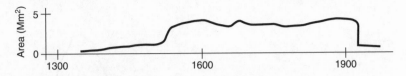

Note: 1 megameter = 1,000 km; 1 sq. megameter (Mm²) = 390,000 sq. miles.

FIGURE 2.4 The Ottoman Parabola.
Source: Rein Taagepera, "Expansion and Contraction Patterns of Large Polities: Context for Russia," International Studies Quarterly 41 (1997): 483–84.

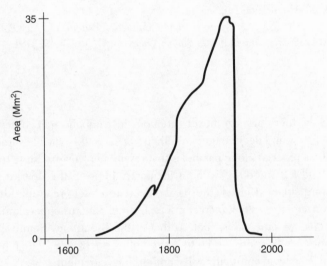

Note: 1 megameter = 1,000 km; 1 sq. megameter (Mm²) = 390,000 sq. miles.

FIGURE 2.5 The British Parabola.
Source: Rein Taagepera, "Expansion and Contraction Patterns of Large Polities: Context for Russia," International Studies Quarterly 41 (1997): 484.

turies. Finally, not unlike the Arabs and Mongols of earlier times, the British and the French (figures 2.5 and 2.6) expanded rapidly and enormously in 1750–1800, reached their peak a century later, and then lost it all within several decades of the twentieth century.

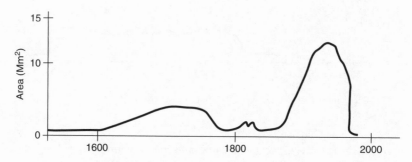

Note: 1 megameter = 1,000 km; 1 sq. megameter (Mm²) = 390,000 sq. miles.

FIGURE 2.6 The French Parabola.
Source: Rein Taagepera, "Expansion and Contraction Patterns of Large Polities: Context for Russia," *International Studies Quarterly* 41 (1997): 482, 484.

Clearly, there are significant variations in parabolic trajectories. Some empires grow and decline quickly; others appear to do so at a leisurely pace; still others proceed along parabolas that resemble plateaus. None rose, persisted, and fell smoothly, without temporary blips on the upward, flat, or downward slopes. Indeed, the parabolas more closely resemble the long-term movement of stock market prices. Overall patterns conceal numerous deviations; in some cases, such as that of the Byzantines (figure 2.7), the deviations can be quite substantial, resembling stocks with a "high beta." As Warren Treadgold summarizes Byzantium's development:

> The years after 284 brought major reforms, including the administrative division between East and West, that mark the beginning of the Byzantine period. Although the West soon resumed its decline and disappeared, the history of the East was less simple, with many declines and recoveries. These are apparent from the East's gains and losses of territory. . . . For the East, [figure 2.7] shows a moderate loss between 300 and 450, the result of defeats by the Persians and Huns. Then a major gain occurred, as much of the former western empire was reconquered by the emperor Justinian. Justinian's gains disappeared by 620, because of new invasions by the Germans, Persians, and Avars.

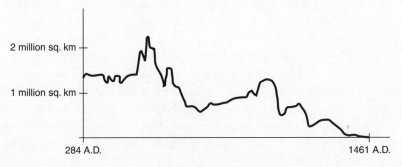

Note: 1,000,000 sq. km = 390,000 sq. miles.

FIGURE 2.7 Territorial Extent of the Byzantine Empire.
Source: Warren Treadgold, A History of the Byzantine State and Society (Palo Alto, Calif.: Stanford University Press, 1997), p. 8.

By 750 another major loss occurred, as the Arabs conquered a large part of Byzantine territory. But this second decline was made good by 1050, when after many reconquests the empire was scarcely smaller than it had been in 300 or 620, and slightly larger than it had been in 450. Then came another severe decline, caused by losses to the Seljuk Turks. Interrupted by a partial recovery, this decline lasted until 1204, when Constantinople fell to the Fourth Crusade, and the provinces that remained under Greek rule were divided among several successor states. Finally the main empire and the smaller Greek states recovered for a time, before shrinking to nothing by 1461, conquered by the Ottoman Turks.[6]

Treadgold's brief account of the decline of the eastern Roman Empire reminds us that, on the one hand, no theory of imperial decline can account for contingencies in general and such momentous contingencies as the Fourth Crusade in particular and that, on the other hand, the actual trajectory of decline cannot possibly be the smooth process that the image of a parabola conveys. Byzantium experienced a variety of ups and downs in the course of its existence; only over time, and in the aggregate, can we plausibly say that its slope was negative and thus that its trajectory was parabolic.

Accounting for these ups and downs, as Taagepera, Christopher Chase-Dunn, and Thomas Hall attempt to do—by arguing, for instance, that empires have gotten larger over time or that the longer it takes for empires to grow, the longer it will take for them to decline—is not my goal.[7] Nor, as I have already argued in chapter 1, can—or should—it be. Even though a theory of everything is beyond our grasp, we are not therefore condemned to abject modesty. That the trajectories of actual empires approximate parabolas permits us to treat parabolic trajectories as baselines, as something *like* algorithmically compressible, virtually lawlike, empirical generalizations.[8] They permit us to claim that rise, persistence, and decline are the norm and thus to argue, plausibly and persuasively, that nonattrition and collapse are deviations from the norm. As a result, we are entitled, first, to explain parabola-like trajectories of decline in terms of some endogenous feature of empire—such as structure—and, second, to account for nonattrition and especially collapse in terms of intervening variables, exogenous factors, and the like.

We could of course insist that parabolic trajectories are the exception and that collapse is the rule. For a structural theory, however, the resulting theoretical claim, that collapse is business as usual while attrition is not, would lead us into a cul de sac. Chapter 1 has already noted that structural theories require exogenous events to account for collapse. If collapse were the norm, the theory would be placed in the untenable position of having to explain not the rule (i.e., its own theoretical domain) but the exceptions to it. Such a denouement would force us to abandon a structural approach for one that is more agency oriented, choice centered, and intentionalist. Bad leaders would, accordingly, lose empires by making bad decisions and bad choices.[9] But as agency, choice, and intention have their own well-nigh fatal flaws, we would be back to our starting point. If so, treating parabolas as the norm and trying to explain decline in structural terms may be, once again, less bad than the alternative; in any case, it certainly seems to entail the construction of fewer face-saving epicycles.

Bringing Totalitarianism Back In

Because the analysis that follows rests on the structural isomorphism between empires and totalitarian states, it may be worth acknowledging that I fully appreciate that totalitarianism is a highly contested concept that—like empire—has been in academic disrepute for many years.[10] Does this unsavory reputation doom any explanatory enterprise that draws on totalitarianism for inspiration and respectability? Only if the concept or term truly terrifies us or only if we believe that all criticism is, merely by virtue of its having appeared, infallible.

Neither stance is justifiable. As a concept, totalitarianism is no better—and no worse—than any other concept. It can, argues Giovanni Sartori, be constructed badly or used unproductively or infused with political content, but so can every other concept.[11] One is fully entitled to hate the totalitarian concept but not because it is inherently hateful. One may also hate the term, but replacing it with an adequate substitute—*shmo*talitarianism perhaps?—is then imperative. As to totalitarianism's critics, they are, like all critics, fallible. We have as little reason to reject totalitarianism as a concept because a generation of scholars at one time rejected it as we have to accept the concept because a different generation accepted it.[12] We would be ill advised to reify any slice of academic time. In this case as in every other, the appropriate question should be whether the critique, or the endorsement, was justified.

As I have argued elsewhere, much of the critique centered on the descriptive inappropriateness of ascribing to the post-Stalinist USSR all the features of totalitarianism developed by Carl Friedrich and Zbigniew Brzezinski.[13] Obviously, if totalitarian states must be terroristic, nonterroristic states cannot be totalitarian. Another strand of criticism, with regard to both Hitler's Germany and Stalin's USSR, pointed to the obvious: that the defining characteristics of totalitarianism—in particular, the notion of the state as a monolith or behemoth—were not as sharply present in either system as the ideal type seemed to require.[14] This observation, although true, missed the boat entirely: no set of defining characteristics of anything can ever apply—completely, fully, totally, and absolutely—to some empirical situation.[15] All concepts are ideal-type constructs that always only approximate life. Seen in this light, determining the empirical referent of the concept of choice is, for instance, no less difficult than finding a real live totalitarian state. I may be able to isolate people, neural impulses, words, quizzical expressions, and bodily movements, but where, exactly, among all these things is choice?[16] The last critique of the totalitarian model—that it could not explain change—was both wrongheaded and wrong. To the extent that the model's supporters claimed to be able to explain persistence, to accuse them of not accounting for change was simply unfair. But the critique is also wrong, because, as Karl Deutsch showed, totalitarianism can explain change.[17]

Deutsch and Decay

Empires "work" when resources flow from the periphery to the core and back to the periphery (*P-C-P*). Empires cease to work when these flows are disrupted and resources remain in the periphery or in the core or in both. Naturally, all political systems work when resources flow efficiently and do not work when they flow inefficiently. Inasmuch as empires as empires are defined by a peculiar kind of structure that also defines the flow of resources, however, the efficient flow of resources is of overwhelming importance to the stability—or self-maintenance—of empires.[18] As a Deutschian perspective would lead us to argue, the efficient flow of resources presupposes adequate information about the resources available in the periphery, about the agencies that channel them to the core and back to the periphery, and about the ends that the resources are supposed to meet. That is, the effective functioning of empire entails information aggregation about the empire *and* about the core state, the peripheral administration, and their relationship: imperial elites must be informed about the condition of their territories, about both sets of bureaucracies, and, most important perhaps, about resource flows from periphery to core to periphery.

In turn, information aggregation and resource distribution presuppose an information-gathering and information-processing apparatus: that is, an effective state in the core and an effective administration in the periphery. Regardless of the size and overall tasks of that apparatus, its ability to function presupposes information about itself. Indeed, information about that apparatus is no less critical than information about the empire to effective decision making in the core and efficient *P-C-P* resource flows. It is here—in the relationship between information aggregation and the information-gathering and -processing apparatus—that a systemic contradiction is lodged. For if information about the information-gathering and information-processing apparatus is not collected, aggregate information will always be incomplete and especially so with respect to the machinery on which it depends. If that information is collected, the information-gathering machinery will grow in complexity in order to gather and process information about the empire and itself. Thus the more the machinery grows and systemic complexity increases, the greater the imperial system's requirement of information and resources. But the greater the information and resource needs of the imperial state and the peripheral administration, the more effective the information-gathering and resource-processing apparatus must be, the more information it must aggregate, and the greater the information and resource needs of the core become. Like oversized automobiles, empires greedily consume the fuel that keeps them going. Indeed, the further empires go, the more information and resources they need. Should such gas-guzzling behavior prove to be unsustainable, empires will be in trouble. Should an empire's growing information and resource needs be incompatible with its own structurally induced incapacity to meet them, the empire will, inescapably, fall victim to a systemic contradiction that will, in the long run, force it to wither away.[19]

At this point the structural isomorphism between empires and totalitarian states becomes crucial to my argument. Totalitarian states of the kind discussed by Deutsch are, as I have already emphasized, far more intrusive than empires—civil societies and market economies are inconceivable in the former but perfectly possible, indeed commonplace, in the latter[20]—but both systems have a distinctly hublike structure. Totalitarian states have a functional structure, involving a core elite and state and functionally defined peripheral elites and agencies—which, obviously, happen to be located in particular places. Empires have a territorial structure, involving a core elite and state and territorially defined peripheral elites and societies. Imperial peripheries are thus geographically bounded areas inhabited by distinct populations; totalitarian peripheries are territorially clustered institutions sustained by distinct elites, classes, or groups. The units comprising the two structures are thus quite different, but the structures are, as figure 2.8 illustrates, *identical*.

The USSR, as the world's only totalitarian empire, arguably represents as pure a structural example of both empire and totalitarianism as one can imagine. The "circular flow of power" that characterized Communist rule exactly mirrored the imperial rule that the core party-state exerted over the republics. In both cases, the Politburo and general secretary made decisions that party and state organs at lower levels voted upon, invariably endorsed, and implemented. The totalitarian side of party rule was functional, extending into organizations, workplaces, and homes; the imperial side was territorial, extending to geographic agglomerations of functional units known as satellites, republics, provinces, and the like. Empire and totalitarianism re-

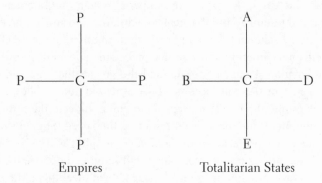

Note: C = core; P = periphery, and A, B, D, and E are different clusters of institutions.

FIGURE 2.8 Structure of Empires and Totalitarian States

inforced each other precisely because they had identical structures and so neatly overlapped.[21] As Valerie Bunce puts it,

> The power of the Soviet Union over its client state in Eastern Europe was secured through bilateral ties controlled by the Soviet Union; through Soviet regional dominance in ideology, political authority, national security, markets, and primary products; and through the Soviet role as a regional hegemon defining and defending the boundaries of the bloc and monopolizing interactions between the bloc and the international system. The Soviet bloc, therefore, was highly centralized and radial in its structure—much as was the case with domestic socialism and, for that matter, empires.[22]

That a variety of scholars writing about the USSR and other communist states have shown how the structure of totalitarianism leads to decay is thus of obvious significance to my case.[23] Włodzimierz Brus's analysis of a centrally planned economy summarizes the general argument:

> With the economic targets growing more and more complex and the list of priorities broadening, the chances diminish of meeting conditions favouring the effective operation of a strictly centralized organization of a planned economy. An attempt at keeping such an organi-

zation alive . . . may lead to diminishing efficiency. . . . It is to be expected that the central level, under the heavy burden of growing current problems, may lose its ability to concentrate on main macroeconomic questions. . . . The effectiveness of decentralization becomes enhanced.[24]

The most important contribution to the theory of totalitarian decay belongs to Deutsch. In an article published in 1954, Deutsch constructed an ideal-type "totalitarian decision system," a key function of which, "unity of command and of intelligence, requires some machinery either to insure a single source of decision, or a set of arrangements or devices to insure consistency of decisions among several sources."[25] Crucial to his scheme is what I have called the core: "A single source of decisions is in effect an arrangement by which all important incoming information available to the system is channeled to a point where it can be confronted with data recalled from a single integrated memory pool."[26] Deutsch then went on to show how such a system necessarily had a "limited capacity of centralized decision-making," with the result that it would be "overloaded with decisions with which it can no longer cope, except at the price of either intolerable delays or an increasing probability of potentially critical mistakes."[27] Equally debilitating was the concomitant "instability of hierarchical power"—that is, of the hublike structure. As Deutsch writes,

> The difficulties that militate against the viability of any permanent system of totalitarian centralization are paralleled, in a sense, by the difficulties in the way of any permanent hierarchical distribution of power. A hierarchy of power requires that all power should be located at the apex of a pyramid, and that all power should lead downward in terms of a transitive chain of command, transmitting orders from the single power holder or the few power holders at the top to the many soldiers or policemen at the bottom. However, every such pyramid of power is inherently unstable. To maintain transitivity it must be steered by orders coming from the apex. Yet the shortest communication routes to all relevant sub-centers and sub-assemblies of power is not from the apex, but from some location farther down.[28]

His conclusion strikes an especially resonant chord: "In the long run there is thus perhaps inherent in every totalitarian system of government a tendency either toward overloading of its central facilities for the making of decisions, or toward an automatic corrosion of its original centralized structure and its disintegration into increasingly separate parts."[29]

Deutsch's theory is structural: it focuses exclusively on the relationships between and among the units comprising a totalitarian system, and it eschews completely all reference to agency, choice, and intention. Equally important, Deutsch's theory has been proved "right," or as right as any theory can be: "If similar considerations should apply to the totalitarian regimes of Russia and China . . . then we might expect the 1970's or 1980's to bring a slowing of the expansive pressure from these two regimes, or a growing divergence of policies between them, or among some of their constituent regions, or some combination of all these changes, leading in either case to a diminution in 'classic' patterns of totalitarian behavior."[30] About forty-five years after his article appeared, the totalitarian states of east-central and eastern Europe fell apart for just the reasons he adduced. Moreover, the history of post-Stalinist communist states can persuasively be interpreted as a ceaseless struggle to deal with the very pathologies Deutsch identified.

The gist of my theoretical claim therefore comes down to these propositions:

- Empires and totalitarian states are structurally isomorphic.
- Structural theories of breakdown in general and of imperial decay in particular are less unpersuasive than agency-oriented, choice-centered, intentionalist accounts.
- Deutsch's theory is persuasive with respect to totalitarian states.
- A successful structural theory such as Deutsch's resembles a weak version of a covering law and, eo ipso, applies to other structurally isomorphic systems—namely, empires.
- Deutsch's theory of totalitarian degeneration is thus a theory of imperial decay.

In brief, because empires and totalitarian states are structurally identical, the structurally generated pathologies identified by Deutsch's theory affect imperial systems no less than they affect totalitarian states.

We now have the final piece of our theoretical puzzle. Johan Galtung highlighted the importance of structure; Taagepera established that all empires would, ceteris paribus, follow a parabolic course of decline. Deutsch provides the theoretical underpinnings for Taagepera's algorithm. We can now claim—with all the tentativeness that theory in general and structural theory in particular requires of us—that empires follow the course of a downward-sloping parabola because imperial structure produces decay. We still have to get from decay—the loosening of C-P ties—to attrition, the actual loss of peripheral territories, but the process, as I demonstrate shortly, is relatively straightforward once decay is in place.

Attrition

Although uneven in its effects, decay appears to proceed inexorably. Empires, like totalitarian states, experience, in Deutsch's language, either "overload" in the core or "disintegration" in the periphery or, most likely, both. Overload disrupts the efficient flow of resources from the periphery to the core and back to the periphery. As resources remain lodged in the periphery and/or core, the "centralized structure" experiences "corrosion" and begins to disintegrate into "increasingly separate parts."

Geoffrey Parker makes the same point: "A further characteristic of the period of decline concerns the spatial distribution of economic power. This entails a shift of the state's economic centre of gravity away from its historic core to a new economic centre located elsewhere in its territory. . . . As a result of this an entirely new centre of population emerges which is likely to have very different social and cultural values from those of the core state."[31] Just such a shift occurred in the western Roman Empire. "Boundaries, physical and spiritual, were changing and being redefined," writes G. W. Bowersock. "The centers were being moved; and the relegations of imperial authority from Rome to Constantinople, and ultimately to Milan, Aquileia, and Ravenna in the north and west, are also metaphors for the tendency to move toward the periphery."[32] Indeed, the barbarianization of the empire was, in this sense, really tantamount to the emergence of autonomous peripheries and a weak core. Barbarians not only seized control of outlying provincial administrations; they also provided the bulk of the armies stationed in those regions.[33] But, according to Geir Lundestad, "once lower units are formed, it appears that sooner or later they almost inevitably will compete with the imperial center."[34] Indeed, as some peripheries develop complementarities and some P-P-P relationships become more efficient than the imperial norm, P-C-P, a growing harmony of interests between periphery

and periphery will supplant the harmony of interests that earlier characterized core and periphery.

As the hublike structure changes—and the "wheel" progressively loses its
spokes and gains a rim—the empire becomes susceptible to attrition. Overloaded and disintegrating, empires will, like decayed totalitarian states, fail
to keep pace with improvements in technology and thus to modernize.[35]
With skewed resource flows and technological backwardness in place, the
state debt is likely to grow at the same time as bureaucracies become parasitic
and state decline sets in. Militarily weakened and bureaucratically bloated
core states will be less able to meet challenges to their rule. Sooner or later,
they will lose bits and pieces of territory as a result of outside aggression or
internally driven "liberation struggles."[36] Kaufman notes:

> Things . . . spiral downward. The downward spirals would set off chain
> reactions. . . . Under these conditions, the central organs would have
> found it increasingly difficult to maintain adequate defense forces as
> well as to preserve internal order and maintain large-scale public
> works. Bandits, raiders, and other freebooters from beyond the perim-
> eters of the polities could roam more freely, but most of all, adjacent
> political systems would be tempted to invade and seize territory.[37]

Historically, wars have been business as usual for empires, as for all great
powers. We may not be able to predict when they will occur, but we do
know that they have occurred, with greater and lesser degrees of intensity,
destructiveness, and scope throughout all recorded history, including the
twentieth century.[38] Ceteris paribus, vigorous empires will be able to hold
their own in any military conflict short of a cataclysmic war; decaying empires, in contrast, will not. They will win some wars, lose others, and barely
scrape by in most. Sooner or later, parts of the empire will be lost to competitors or break away.

Liberation struggles are also likely to occur and to succeed in decaying
empires. As the disharmony of interests, informality of rule, and the possibility of P-P-P and Z-P-Z relations grow, some peripheries will attempt to
wrest more autonomy or even independence from the core. Because Britain's American colonies had developed extensive economic and political
linkages long before 1776, they could mount organized opposition to His
Majesty's imposition of various taxes and successfully rebel.[39] Nationalism,
patriotism, and the quest for cultural authenticity need not be present; it

suffices that, to put the case metaphorically, conditions be ripe, peripheral elites seek their day in the sun, windows of opportunity be open, and the core be distracted.[40] As with wars, some struggles will fail and some will succeed; over time, however, peripheries will manage to secede.

With regard to both wars and liberation struggles, core elites may lose contests or they may choose not to fight for occupied territories and resist liberation struggles, thereby effectively abandoning peripheries to their fate. Whatever the case, the real choice—if indeed it is a choice—is not *to end empire* but *not to resist imperial decay*. Withdrawal in this sense is not so much a choice as the long-term culmination of adjustments, choices, and nonchoices—the many straws that broke the camel's back—that in retrospect appear to amount to a momentous decision to abandon long-held territories. Or withdrawal is the immediate effect of overwhelming circumstances that literally force the imperial power to step back: it is thus not so much a choice as a "recognition of necessity."[41] Bernard Porter's analysis of the British retreat from empire is instructive:

[The fall of the Empire] was probably inevitable. It was certainly un-avoidable from the viewpoint of power, because as a world power the Empire would have had to muster the same amounts of material and military power as the Soviet Union and the USA after World War II. Britain could not measure up against these two powers. Some impe-rialists had believed that this would have been possible had the enor-mous natural and human resources of the Empire been utilized more efficiently, but that would have required a deeper and broader imperial engagement than the British people and their imperial brothers, sisters, and subordinates had ever shown. There had never been an engage-ment for a common, clear vision, for a goal and the determined means for reaching it. The manner in which the Empire had evolved—ac-cidental, minimal, and without much consideration or conse-quence—made it impossible.[42]

Decaying Empires

Although the sequence of steps culminating in decay and attrition was derived logically, it does correspond to the composite story of imperial de-cline with which I began this chapter. As Taagepera's parabolas lead us to expect, not every empire will go through such recognizably discrete stages. Moreover, the timing of decay and attrition cannot be predicted: all we can say is that they will set in, probably in the long run. Even so, we expect the histories of empires to correlate, even if imperfectly, with this logically constructed narrative. The following examples provide some grounds for optimism.

Later Han China (23–220 A.D.) experienced decay as the result of two mutually reinforcing trends. First was a growing conflict between the imperial throne and the literati, who "served as cultural carriers and social critics as well as bureaucrats and community leaders."[43] In particular, writes Cho-yun Hsu,

> the literati acquired intellectual autonomy by systematizing knowledge, which gave them the power to legitimize the regime. Self-regeneration through bureaucracy and control of economic resources such as land gave them sufficient self-confidence that they became indispensable to the state. Their demand that the political authority meet their standard, in addition to their obvious autonomy, was enough to alienate the throne from their intimidating influence.[44]

Second was the competition between the core and the peripheral areas that had grown "in a general trend of demographic redistribution and economic development."[45] According to Cho-yun Hsu,

> In the peripheral areas social power most likely would be concentrated within small groups of elites, since leadership tended to be monopolized by the local establishment. . . . Regional differentiation was strengthened by the difficulty of incorporating peripheral areas into the national resource-flow network and was further bolstered by the Confucian focus on local concerns, encouraged by the constant tension and frequent conflicts between the literati and the throne.[46]

With generalized decay as the backdrop, the Han empire became enervated by a "decade of continuous conflicts" (141–151 A.D.) with its version of Rome's barbarians, the Ch'iang tribes, and the devastating Yellow Turban peasant revolt initiated by the warlord Tung Cho in 188 A.D. Significantly, an earlier struggle against the Xiongnu nomads had been far more costly than the war against the Ch'iang, but the empire, still unaffected by decay, had survived intact.[47] In 220 the last Han emperor was deposed, and China split into three kingdoms.

The Roman Empire, according to Michael Doyle, was "bound to weaken. The army and the bureaucracy grew to be enormous organizations supported by the declining, taxable, productive part of the population." Worse, "the west was tending to see a concentration of property and income within an ever smaller landlord class that was reorganizing economic life into near-feudal patterns." As a result, "when the state sought resources from society in the west, it had to grant special concessions to the powerful rich who not only owned the land but staffed the bureaucracy, and each new state demand progressively increased the enfeudalization of the economy." In the end, "a vicious circle of privatization and tax avoidance left the state impoverished, the rich wealthy, and the mass of the people destitute and dependent."[48] Similarly, Alexander Demandt isolates four factors that transformed the "coercive state" (*Zwangsstaat*) into a "giant with clay feet." First was the "bureaucratic state apparatus itself, which was either unable or unwilling to work in the spirit of the Emperor." Second was the "large landowners," who resisted paying taxes and providing recruits. Third was the church, which "removed itself from the directives of the Emperor." Fourth was the military, which developed its own interests.[49]

Although the imperial administration consisting of a "rudimentary apparatus of officialdom" did not match the "dimensions of the empire," decay assumed alarming proportions only in the third century A.D., as rebellious frontier troops routinely placed their commanders on the imperial throne.[50] In turn, barbarians attacked, while the Persians attempted to reconquer Mesopotamia. Conditions stabilized after the emperor Aurelian defeated the Goths in 268–269 and withdrew from Dacia while redeploying his forces in Egypt and Gaul. Diocletian and Constantine reformed the army and bureaucracy, in both the core and periphery, but at great cost to the economy. The peasants suffered, while landowners and noblemen generally succeeded in evading taxation and increasing their holdings. "The contrast between the formidable weight of the Roman military machine and its inefficiency is thus striking," writes Philippe Contamine.

> The Roman army was an impressive organization, impeccably structured in theory, but which in practice kept seizing up. The Emperors . . . were unable to use the opportunities represented by facility of communication, an abundance of information and rapidity in the dis-

patch of orders. Furthermore, the bureaucracy which sustained their efforts was small, easily overloaded or discouraged; it expected only delays and adopted an obstructive role.[51]

The relocation of the imperial court to Constantinople in 330 may have consolidated Constantine's rule, but it also diminished Rome's stature and enabled military commanders in the west to act autonomously. The barbarianization of the army proceeded apace, partly in response to the declining number of available recruits and partly as a means of appeasing potential invaders. Revolts and civil wars left the western empire vulnerable to full-scale attrition. The Alans, Sueves, and Vandals overran Gaul in 406–407; the Visigoths sacked Rome in 410; Attila the Hun raided the Danube provinces in 435–453; the Vandals captured Carthage in 439; and the Ostrogoths occupied Pannonia in 454.[52]

The Ottomans reached the height of their power in the sixteenth and seventeenth centuries. Soon thereafter the central government became increasingly ineffective, military and technological modernization lagged behind that of other powers, and centrifugal tendencies multiplied. "The bureaucratic and religious institutions all over the Empire," writes Bernard Lewis, "suffered a catastrophic fall in efficiency and integrity, which was accentuated by the growing change in methods of recruitment, training and promotion. . . . The same fall in professional and moral standards can be seen, though perhaps in less striking form, in the different ranks of the religious and judicial hierarchy. Most striking of all was the decline of the Ottoman armed forces."[53] Small wonder, continues Lewis, that

> the central government ceased to exercise any check or control over agriculture and village affairs, which were left to the unchecked rapacity of the tax-farmers, the leaseholders, and the bailiffs of court nominees. During the seventeenth century some of the more permanently established lease-holders began to coalesce with the landowners into a new landed aristocracy—the *ayan-imemleket* or country notables, whose appearance and usurpation of some of the functions and authority of government were already noted at the time.[54]

The "greatest portion"—approximately two-thirds—of government revenues came from the tithes and livestock taxes paid by peasants.[55] Local elites not only contributed little to the state budget; they also profited handsomely from their roles as tax farmers and tithe collectors.[56]

For most of the late Ottoman Empire (1876–1909) elites struggled to cover mounting expenditures with insufficient tax revenues and the accumulation of state debt. One major drain on the budget was the growth in and transformation of the Sublime Porte into a modern bureaucracy.[57] At the same time, military outlays comprised about 40 percent of total budget expenditures.[58] The large sums spent on the armed forces and gendarmerie notwithstanding, the Ottoman military continued to lag behind its west European competitors. According to Parker,

> There were three important respects in which the military revolution was imperfectly practiced by Europe's most dangerous neighbor. First, and best-known, was the Ottoman decision to build their military big, whereas the Western powers concentrated on increasing the mobility and numbers of their guns. . . . [Second], Ottoman troops were expert imitators, but poor innovators. . . . [A] third source of Ottoman inadequacy in the military sphere [was] metallurgical inferiority.[59]

The eighteenth century witnessed the beginnings of attrition. The territories north of the Black Sea and the Crimea fell to Russia; the Ottomans lost Hungary and parts of Serbia and Wallachia to the Habsburgs; Iran exerted pressure in the east. Matters only deteriorated in the nineteenth century. As the Serbs rebelled in 1804 and 1815, the Greeks pursued a war of independence in 1822–1830, and Egypt became quasi-independent under Muhammad Ali, the Ottoman realm also came under increased pressure from Russia, Austria, Britain, and France, which seized substantial chunks of Ottoman territory in northern Africa and the Balkans. The Congress of Berlin in 1878 crowned Ottoman humiliation by partitioning Bulgaria, slicing off Bosnia-Hercegovina, granting Serbia, Romania, and Montenegro independence, and handing control of Tunisia to France and Cyprus to Britain.[60]

Treadgold notes that in the eleventh and twelfth centuries "the wealth and power of the [Byzantine] empire's landholding and commercial classes increased. . . . The magnates' share of land and official posts continued to grow until the empire began to have a hereditary ruling class, as before it had not. . . . Because such men were harder to rule than ordinary subjects, the power of even the most determined and capable emperors tended to diminish, or at least become harder to use."[61] George Ostrogorsky is harsher in his judgment: "The wealthy landlords absorbed the property of peasant and soldier, turning the former owners into dependents. Thus the very foundations on which Byzantium had built ever since its revival in the seventh century were swept away, with the result that the strength of the armed forces and of the revenue declined, and the consequent impoverishment weakened the military power of the state still further."[62] In time, although "Byzantium still clung to its imperial unity, . . . the structure of the state steadily disintegrated and the relationship between the center and the provinces grew rapidly looser."[63]

Treadgold's estimates of Byzantine budgets (table 2.1) also show that expenditures for the bureaucracy and the military gradually increased in the last five hundred years of the empire's existence and, with the exception of the late sixth and seventh centuries, were on the rise since the empire's inception.

As the "many exemptions enjoyed by the big landowners diminished the revenue from the land tax" and Byzantine control of Mediterranean trade was ceded to the Venetians and Genoese, "Byzantium's financial ruin was," according to Charles Diehl, "inevitable." As a result, writes Diehl,

> since the Byzantine government clung to its tradition of magnificence and display . . . and was determined to keep up appearances, it found increasing difficulty in balancing revenue and expenditure. Attempts were made to economize, regardless of the Empire's safety. Thus from the end of the thirteenth century the fleet . . . was allowed to decay,

TABLE 2.1 Bureaucracy and Military as Percentage of Byzantine Budgets, 300–1321

Year	300	450	518	540	565	641	668	775	842	959	1025	1321
Bureaucracy (%)	9	10	9	10	13	13	25	21	16	15	14	n/a
Military (%)	81	69	65	71	72	78	60	58	65	69	70	68
Total (%)	90	79	74	81	85	91	85	79	81	84	84	n/a

Source: Warren Treadgold, A History of the Byzantine State and Society (Palo Alto, Calif.: Stanford University Press, 1997), pp. 145, 277, 412, 576, 843. Percentages were calculated on the basis of Treadgold's data. Military expenditures include the pay of bodyguards, soldiers, and oarsmen; uniforms, arms, and rations; fodder, horses, and mules; campaigns; and other military expenses.

on the pretext that its upkeep was a needless expense. . . . Other
essentials such as fortresses and armaments were likewise pared away.[64]

As Franz Georg Maier summarizes the process:

The instances of internal weakness in the late Byzantine state are not
to be underrated. In a more and more disintegrating political system
with declining financial and military resources a frequently minimally
capable government attempted without success to master religious
troubles, conflicts over the throne, and civil wars internally and to
prevent further losses of territory externally. The emperor became increasingly dependent on the large noble families, whose growing independence finally undermined his own position.[65]

Starting with the eleventh century, attrition proved unstoppable. The Seljuk Turks advanced relentlessly from the east, and by 1300 most of Asia
Minor was in their hands. In turn, the Crusaders destabilized the empire.
Indeed, the "Fourth Crusade shattered a tradition of unified government in
the Aegean basin that dated back to the Roman Republic, and wrecked
institutions that were as old as Diocletian and Constantine I."[66] Rebellions
and civil wars became increasingly commonplace, especially in the Balkans.[67] Finally, the Ottoman encirclement of what remained of Byzantium
culminated in the fall of Constantinople in 1453 and Trebizond in 1461.

The American colonies held by Britain and Spain followed similar paths
of increasing autonomy vis-à-vis their respective cores. Doyle finds the "root
cause for the collapse of the English empire in America" in England's failure
to "create a politically autonomous center of empire in the metropole."
Because the "colonists had become accustomed more to suzerainty than to
empire in the eighteenth century," they perceived England's attempt to establish "full bureaucratic control" as a threat to "traditional liberties" and
resisted.[68] The fall of the Spanish Empire was an even more clear-cut case
of decay. Doyle provides a useful step-by-step account:

First, there was a deterioration in the efficiency and honesty of the
bureaucracy. Particularism, as in Rome, led to a quasi-feudalization of
bureaucratic posts as offices were sold to creole elites in order to raise
immediate revenue and new offices were created to reward peninsular
Spaniards with colonial spoils. The autonomy of imperial direction

suffered; fewer resources could be mobilized or made available for economic development. . . . Second, the economy of some colonies tended toward ruralization and concentration of property, dissolving ties of economic reciprocity with Spain and leaving only the economic tie of taxation—a chain of servitude. Third, other colonies, among them Cuba, Argentina, and Venezuela, were economically much more dynamic, and as Spain's own economy declined, the constraints of the mercantilist system proved increasingly irksome to colonials. Fourth, the creole elite perceived itself as caught between resentment of Spanish domination and fear of a slave, peasant, or Indian rising.[69]

The attrition of the Spanish Empire in Latin America for the most part involved a concerted series of liberation struggles prompted by two wars. The Thirty Years' War (1618–1648) had resulted in Spain's loss of territory in the Netherlands. No less important, as Renate Pieper points out, was that "Spain came into a deep political, military, and financial crisis as a result of the territorial losses of the Thirty Years War and could no longer therefore send sufficiently trained administrators and troops to Spanish America."[70] That crisis eventually came to a head with Napoleon's invasion of the Iberian Peninsula in 1808. In addition to occupying Spain, Napoleon forced King Ferdinand VII to abdicate and replaced him with his own brother Joseph. At the same time, the Portuguese royal family fled to Brazil. In effect if not in intent, Napoleon subverted both imperial orders. On the one hand, he delegitimized Spanish rule in Latin America—very much in the manner that the Bolshevik coup in late 1917 would later delegitimize Russian imperial rule in the non-Russian borderlands—and provided peripheral elites with the opportunity to pursue their own interests.[71] On the other hand, the flight of Portugal's court transferred the center of imperial rule to a colony and effectively promoted it to the status of a quasi-partner of the former core.

Because creole elites had long since been implicated in a disharmony of interests, it was not surprising that liberation struggles broke out soon after these momentous changes in the core-periphery relationship.[72] Foreshadowing Franz Joseph's later policy toward Hungary, the Portuguese prince regent Dom João granted Brazil the status of a kingdom in 1815. In Spanish America a series of liberators emerged—Simón Bolívar, José de San Martín, and Bernardo O'Higgins were the most prominent—to lead struggles against contintental rule. By the late 1820s almost all peripheral provinces in Latin America had attained independence. Most of Spain's remaining colonies—

the Philippines, Cuba, and Puerto Rico—would be lost to the United States in the 1890s, while Portugal's peripheral holdings in Mozambique, Angola, and Guinea would acquire independence as a result of homegrown liberation struggles in the 1970s.[73]

French and British imperial holdings were lost to a combination of wars and liberation struggles. The Great Depression severely shook France and Britain, leading to massive unemployment and social unrest, radically reducing trade, inducing "business [to] turn inwards," and thereby loosening core ties to their peripheries.[74] In addition, two world wars within three decades strained both empires economically and militarily; the post–World War II emergence of the United States as the world's leading power further constrained Britain and France in their activities throughout the world.[75] Most important perhaps, total war had advanced decay by devastating many of their colonies in North Africa, the Middle East, and Asia and thereby upsetting existing colonial practices, forcing local populations to mobilize in self-defense, and promoting peripheral leaders. Not incidentally, nationalism also took off, to be championed by the world's other great power, the Soviet Union. John Darwin summarizes this process as follows:

> The war produced a dangerous conjuncture of international, domestic and colonial pressures, whose effects were mutually reinforcing. The struggle to uphold their great power position, together with domestic imperatives, left the British no alternative but to pursue colonial policies that were riskier and riskier. At the same time, the very international changes which prompted these policies—the rise of American and Soviet power—also made it progressively more difficult for the British to contain the colonial and semi-colonial unrest their own actions were helping to generate. They increasingly lost the ability to manage the nebulous but potent influence of "world opinion," especially at its principal forum at the United Nations.[76]

The British had already had to contend with nationalist forces in India and Palestine. The former was partitioned, and Pakistan and India gained independence in 1947; Palestine became independent Israel in 1948. Induced by problems at home, cold war rivalries, and nationalist demands abroad, British withdrawal from the Middle East, Asia, and Africa continued and was completed more or lest uneventfully by the 1960s. The French followed suit, especially after their humiliating defeat in Vietnam and costly victory in Algeria proved beyond doubt that their hold on empire was exceedingly tenuous.[77] "To many outside observers," writes Paul Kennedy, "especially the Americans, [the French] attempt to regain the trappings of first-class power status while so desperately weak economically—and so dependent upon American financial support—was nothing more than a *folie des grandeurs*."[78] In sum, writes Charles Tilly, "the situation favored European withdrawal: the USSR had no colonies in the major areas of European colonization, and the United States had few, while the European powers were preoccupied with recovery from the ravages of war."[79] Significantly, although direct rule eventually ended, imperial relations of a more informal kind actually intensified. Both Great Britain and France continued to exert enormous influence on formerly peripheral elites granted nominal independence within a set of relationships that were hegemonic and informal.[80]

Blips and Impossibilities

It is probably impossible to say which form of attrition will affect which empires, and it is certainly impossible to predict when exactly wars or struggles will occur and with whom. Naturally, expansionist neighbors will be more of a threat than nonexpansionist ones, and well-governed empires should experience less discontent and thus fewer internal challenges than poorly governed realms. True enough, perhaps, but the first proposition borders on the obvious and the second on the irrelevant: after all, as the empires under consideration are all decayed, they must, ipso facto, be more or less poorly governed. In the final analysis, we can only say, along with Joseph Tainter, that decay increases significantly the mathematical probability that wars and liberation struggles will, at different points in time, interact with decayed and dissolving imperial systems to produce attrition.[81]

Although we expect all empires inexorably to proceed downward on Taagepera's parabolas, they need not do so with equal alacrity. Adjustments in the resource flow—brought about by policies, leaders, economic and social change, and various contingencies—are inevitable. In particular, increased production—the result of either greater infusions of capital and labor or improvements in technology—could meet the growing resource requirements of the core state. But economic growth, while possible, will not be sustainable beyond the short run. Greater infusions of productive factors are unlikely to be forthcoming as long as resource extraction remains high. To the contrary, we expect the imperial population either to apply itself less or to evade taxation or both, perhaps not immediately but surely over time.[82]

The picture with technologically driven improvements in productivity is more complicated. On the one hand, a resource-hungry state will discourage innovation no less than it will discourage effort. On the other hand, the leaders of a large, intrusive, hypercentralized state—which will return to the scene in chapter 3—could intervene directly in the economy and promote technological change. Whether such a state can sustain such an effort for more than the short run, however, is doubtful.[83] Its own bloatedness militates against the efficient use of resources; its information deficiencies argue against the successful targeting of growth technologies. In sum, we expect some state-driven growth, but we do not expect it to save the day and extricate the empire from its structural dilemmas.[84]

We also expect decay to be affected by the type of empire concerned. First, decay should be greater and more intense in larger empires than in smaller ones. The more peripheries there are, the larger the demands on information aggregation and resource allocation, the greater the likelihood of overload and disintegration.[85] Second, imperial maintenance should consume more resources in discontinuous empires than in continuous ones. Compact empires are easier to defend—the lines of supply are shorter, transportation costs are lower, and administration is simpler. Constantine the Great arguably acted on this principle by dividing the Roman Empire into two administrative halves, thereby ensuring Byzantium's survival for another millennium. As distance translates into higher costs, into more complex and more expensive imperial relationships, discontinuous empires should be especially susceptible to disruptions in resource flows and thus to decay and attrition.[86] Third, informal empire is tantamount to the institutionalization of greater resource retention by peripheral elites. As a result, we expect the resource squeeze to afflict informal empires sooner than formal or less informal ones.

How far will attrition proceed in any particular case? Structural theories have no way of knowing. An empire could, like those of Rome or Constantinople, disappear completely; it could contract to encompass only the core, as happened to the Ottomans and the Habsburgs; or it could stabilize at some size larger than the core. Any one of these individual outcomes can be explained historically, but any overall generalization would flirt with some notion of optimal state size. All we can say with any degree of certainty is that the more empires contract, the smaller and less discontinuous they become. It follows that attrition should slow down as empires decay and become progressively more compact and that empires may stabilize at some smaller size that may or may not correspond to an integrated state or some approximation of a nation-state. Byzantium may illustrate this dynamic, having survived as little more than Constantinople and its suburbs for about a century.

3   Imperial Collapse

Although empires do appear to slide down Taagepera's parabolas in the right way and for the right reasons, it is, alas, also true that attrition does not always follow on the heels of decay. However discomfiting theoretically, this fact should not surprise us too much: decay is internal to the workings of empire and as such is more or less indifferent to exogenous goings-on. In contrast, attrition—as a function of war and externally abetted liberation struggles—depends at least in part on an empire's overall geopolitical position and should as a result be susceptible to a variety of intervening variables. Even so, nonattrition is, if not a puzzle, then certainly an anomaly. We shall have to account for it in a manner that pays tribute to the priority of decay *and* that treats exceptions to the rule in a way that either minimizes, if not fully eliminates, the unpredictability of exogenous factors or incorporates them meaningfully into the explanatory narrative.

The three exceptions I consider are the USSR, Austria-Hungary, and Romanov Russia. All decayed, and all experienced various forms of the pathologies identified in chapter 2. But none experienced attrition or as much attrition as we might—counterfactually—have expected. A perfectly plausible reason is that all three empires had actually decayed very little. Taagepera's parabolas show that the Soviet and Russian realms had reached their maximum territorial extent just before they collapsed. One could argue that attrition would have taken place had these empires not encountered cataclysms that destroyed them prematurely, before they began *really* to decay. That Austria had lost much territory in the nineteenth century weakens these claims. So too one could note that the USSR collapsed as the result not of some outside cataclysm such as war but of an internal stress surge, perestroika.[1] If so, decay must have been highly advanced for a reform program to have destroyed a superpower. These counterarguments can, of course, in turn be countered and, in the final analysis, all one can do is suggest why one's account is both plausible and, perhaps, more plausible. And that entails making the case historically for advanced decay in the Soviet, Habsburg, and Romanov contexts.

The Soviet Empire

The appropriation of lands, at first of the non-Russian territories and later of the east-central European states, took place in the first three decades of the Soviet imperial experiment, between 1917 and 1948. By the early 1950s it appeared that the Soviet empire had achieved near-monolithic unity. The non-Russian republics were bludgeoned into submission during the 1930s, while the satellites, with the exception of Yugoslavia, were Stalinized after the war. Soviet imperial history after Stalin's death, however, is largely a record of steady, and occasionally very convulsive, decay. Three trends stand out.

First, in contrast to the Habsburg and Romanov realms, which underwent rapid and dynamic economic growth in the last decades of their existence, the Soviet empire experienced steep economic decline.[2] Central planning proved quite incapable of promoting technological modernization. It also engendered a variety of pathologies—statistical padding, the hoarding of resources by factory managers and peripheral elites, the fetishization of production and of quantitative indicators—that severely disrupted periphery-to-core resource flows.[3] These dysfunctional consequences of totalitarianism also encouraged core intervention in local affairs and promoted the growth of the central bureaucracy.

Second, all the peripheries acquired a life of their own in the decades following Stalin's death. Although the Russian core elite retained control, the non-Russian entities in east-central Europe and the USSR developed corporate bureaucracies with regional interests and native intelligentsias with nationalist aspirations. The upshot was that most peripheries witnessed the emergence of local Communist Party machines that ruthlessly pursued their own interests, very often to the detriment of the interests of the core elite or the empire as a whole.[4] Because we expect decay to be most advanced in informally ruled outlying regions—which succumbed, in Timothy Garton Ash's terminology, to "Ottomanization"—it is not surprising that east-central European peripheral elites engaged in a variety of liberation struggles.[5] Official elites led the way in Poland and Hungary in 1956 and in Czechoslovakia in 1968; they attained autonomy for Romania in the 1960s; and they followed the lead of unofficial elites in Poland in 1980 and, finally, in most of east-central Europe in 1989.[6]

Third, the Soviet empire even experienced decline. Although "over 5 million uniformed personnel, some 27,000 nuclear weapons, 55,000 tanks, over 200 army divisions, 6,000 fighter/attack aircraft, 9,000 surface to air missile air defense launchers, almost 300 naval surface warships, and an equal number of attack submarines" were, according to Stephen Meyer, "arrayed against the Western democracies" in the late 1980s, the Soviet military had become increasingly ineffective.[7] Soviet military technology could not keep pace with America's, war planning remained mired in the outdated strategic thinking engendered by World War II, training was inadequate, and morale was low. The occupation of Afghanistan after 1978 amply confirmed that the Soviet armed forces were not as invincible as Western policy makers often assumed them to be. The USSR did possess an enormous nuclear arsenal, but that was of little use in preventing or defeating peripheral challenges to Soviet rule. In sum, advanced economic rot, the insubordination of peripheral elites, and state decline should have produced some attrition, but the Soviet empire experienced no loss of territory in the decades after the break with Yugoslavia. Indeed, the combination of external expansion and internal decline was, as Seweryn Bialer put it, the essence of the "Soviet paradox."[8]

The Habsburg Empire

The Habsburgs experienced substantial attrition in the first seven decades of the nineteenth century. Successive defeats at the hands of Napoleon detached some territories; a series of liberation struggles and wars deprived Vienna of its Italian holdings.[9] Despite rampant decay and extensive decline, however, Austria lost no more territories after 1866, while actually annexing Bosnia-Hercegovina in 1908. This arrested form of attrition is all the more puzzling because, as Robert Kann suggests, the Habsburg empire may have been subject to a process of steady decay from the time it incorporated Bohemia, Moravia, and Hungary in the early part of the sixteenth century.[10] Core control over the crown lands was always tenuous; local diets tended to persist, as did local laws, customs, elites, and their prerogatives. Maria Theresa and Joseph II adopted centralizing reforms with the goal of transforming the empire into some approximation of a Western-style state.[11] Although an efficient bureaucracy was eventually put in place, the core's tug of war with truculent elites in the crown lands continued even after the repressive regime of Francis I. Indeed, according to Kann, "the whole history of the Habsburg monarchy shows a distinct conflict between what may be called the territorial aristocracy in the historico-political entities; namely, those Habsburg lands of independent cultural-political tradition, on the one hand, and the high court nobility at the administrative center of the empire in Vienna on the other."[12]

In 1848, with Vienna besieged by revolutionaries, the provinces in general and Hungary in particular emerged to assert their rights or to make new demands. Franz Joseph's subsequent experiment with neoabsolutism ended with his defeat by Napoleon III at Solferino, while the Kaiser's unwillingness to countenance a looser arrangement for the crown lands came to an end with the *Ausgleich* of 1867, which in essence institutionalized informal rule in Hungary.[13] The terms of the compromise encouraged Hungarian elites to up the autonomist ante every time they renegotiated their relations with Vienna.[14] Moreover, the resulting physical structure of the empire—its division into a moon-shaped Cisleithania and a compact Transleithania dominated by Hungary—effectively demoted Vienna to one link in a long chain of roads, railroads, and telegraph wires and promoted Budapest to the center of its own bailiwick. Indeed, Vienna's disadvantaged location resembled Cuzco's in the Inca realm. "Gradually," writes Istvan Deak, "the administrative machinery was becoming 'national,' with the provincial bureaucracies adapting themselves to the local ethnic-political forces, often quite independently of the national origin of the functionaries themselves."[15] All these changes encouraged interperiphery relations, and especially trade, to grow and the centrifugal tendencies exerted by Magyars, Czechs, Poles, Italians, Serbs, and others to accelerate.[16] Incipient disassemblage and advanced decay reinforced each other, posing a permanent threat to the integrity of the imperial polity until its collapse in 1918.

Austria-Hungary also experienced decline. Napoleon's armies smashed the Kaiser's military at Marengo, Hohenlinden, Austerlitz, and Wagram.

Count Metternich did little to improve Austria's armed forces in the decades that followed, concentrating instead on internal control. The year 1848 exposed the weakness of the state. The military and police proved powerless in the face of revolutionary uprisings, and—much to Friedrich Engels's regret—only the intervention of Russia saved the day.[17] The empire's subsequent military engagements were no less lackluster.[18] The French defeated the Habsburg armies at Solferino in 1859, and the Prussians crushed the Austrians at Sadowa in 1866. Thereafter, the Habsburg armed forces, while resplendent in their uniforms, played mostly an internal policing function and served as a vehicle for integrating the empire's many nationalities.[19] Although the officer corps was competent, the army was generally recognized as being inferior, a point that tiny Serbia was to demonstrate in August 1914.[20]

The Russian Empire

Although the Russian Empire continued to expand almost until its end, it too experienced extensive decay by the end of the nineteenth century and the beginning of the twentieth. One reason for decay was that the centralizing reforms initiated by Peter the Great and continued assiduously by Catherine—which were so alike in spirit to those implemented by the centralizing reformers of the House of Habsburg, Maria Theresa and Joseph II—only partially succeeded in integrating the borderlands, especially those acquired from Poland.[21] Although Peter and Catherine achieved much in the way of transforming Russia into what Marc Raeff calls a "well-ordered police state"—they created an administrative system, assigned regional governors, and rationalized laws throughout the empire—the transformation remained far from complete.[22] Khans ruled Khiva, emirs ruled Bukhara, clans ran the North Caucasus, and traditional elites remained in power in Georgia; the Baltic lands were in the hands of the German nobility; Polish nobles were unrepentant even after two failed insurrections in 1830 and 1860; Finland remained a grand duchy with its own diet and laws.[23] Indeed, Martin Spechler has shown how Finland's relationship with the core had begun to dissolve, as "opportunities to sell sawn timber products at favorable prices to Britain and to buy high-quality manufactured goods from the West favored a decoupling from the Russian Empire."[24]

The Napoleonic wars did not produce collapse, but they did accelerate decay, enabling peripheral elites—Swedes, Baltic Germans, Poles, and others—to lay claim to traditional rights, customs, and prerogatives and expose the "Russian paradox" of simultaneous expansion and state decline. The army epitomized this paradoxical condition. As Walter M. Pinter points out, the overall percentage devoted by the state budget to military expenditures declined by about half "in the age of Catherine the Great, even though the size of the army increased, probably reflect[ing] the very rapid growth in the area and population of the Empire, and the attention and expenditure that Catherine lavished on internal administration." Worse, the size of the army was not matched with appropriate technology. Thus about two-thirds to three-fourths of the total army budget between 1863 and 1913 continued to go toward subsistence items and not weapons and ships. "The reason for Russia's large army," according to Pinter, "was undoubtedly in part inertia, the tradition of simply having a large army, partly the unchanging geographical reality, the great distances and the extensive frontiers that had to be guarded." In addition, Russia needed a large army because its technological backwardness, and especially its lack of a well-developed railroad network, meant that it could not, like more advanced West European states, retain a trained reserve force that could be called up and quickly mobilized in case of war.[25]

That Russia's armed forces succeeded in overwhelming Central Asia and the Caucasus, which joined the empire largely on an informal basis in the nineteenth century, testified to Russia's comparative military strength vis-à-vis its "near abroad." On the other hand, it was clear that Russia was no match for the more advanced Western powers. The tsar's armies beat back Napoleon only with the help of winter, and they proved strong enough to save Vienna from ragtag revolutionary bands in 1848. But the Crimean War and, especially, the 1905 war with Japan showed that the armed forces, while still superior to Kazak nomads, radical students, and Bukharan foot soldiers, were no match for modernized states.[26] Like Austria-Hungary, however, Romanov Russia experienced no attrition despite advanced decay and decline. Instead, it actually expanded.

Imperial Props

As these three cases illustrate, empires need not proceed automatically along the trajectory depicted by Taagepera's parabolas. That trajectory depends on two links—between imperial decay and state decline, and between state decline and attrition—that cannot be taken for granted. Four variables can intervene to arrest decay, decline, and/or attrition.

- A hypercentralized core state can, as in the case of the USSR, prevent peripheral elites from drifting away—not by eliminating the reasons for, or capacity to engage in, drift but by maintaining strict organizational and coercive control over the periphery.
- A favorable geopolitical environment can sustain a declining empire and forestall attrition. In particular, alliances can shield empires, as Wilhelmine Germany shielded Austria-Hungary.
- A favorable geographic location can, as was the case with Romanov Russia, have the same effect as a favorable geopolitical environment.
- Internally generated easy money, like the external support of generous allies, can sustain empire; it permits core elites to sidestep the problem of declining resources and unproductive economies and sustain requisite levels of imperial expenditure.[27] Spain's discovery of silver and gold in the New World was just such a boon, as was the USSR's windfall from the oil embargo of 1973.

As I argue next, these four props are, first, consistent—or, at least, not inconsistent—with the theoretical framework I propose in this book. Second, they address the forms of attrition—wars and liberation struggles—discussed in chapter 2. Third, although these factors may be explained historically, they cannot be predicted. Fourth, because these factors are necessarily impermanent, their longer-term effect may be to make buttressed empires even more prone to shocks and thus to collapse.

1. With respect to theoretical consistency, nothing about a structural theory of imperial decay excludes the importance or relevance of such factors as geography, natural resources, and the broader setting of international relations. The only variable that appears to contravene the model is the notion that an exceedingly top-heavy, hypercentralized state can arrest decay. After all, I had specifically argued that a bloated state *promotes* decay. We can escape this seeming contradiction by, as already noted in chapter 2, splitting hairs—namely, by arguing that a *very* top-heavy state will both advance decay *and*, by virtue of its size, strength, and capacity, temporarily keep peripheral elites from drifting and/or breaking away. Resting on a contradiction, such an outcome is, of course, necessarily unstable and unlikely to be long lasting.

But such an outcome is theoretically conceivable and, as I argue with respect to the USSR, empirically possible.

2. All four intervening variables reduce the chances of attrition. By keeping peripheral elites on a short leash—by means of tight organizational control of their training, appointment, and promotion—a hypercentralized state will prevent them from embarking on interperiphery linkages or alliances with outside polities. A favorable geopolitical environment in general and alliances in particular will effectively reduce the possibility of war and especially of devastating war. Favorable geography—or physical distance from arenas of war or of great-power competition—can also minimize the possibility and/or effect of war. A. H. M. Jones, for instance, attributes the survival of the eastern half of the Roman Empire to the fact that

> strategically the Eastern Empire was, during the fourth and fifth centuries, far better placed than the Western. . . . The barbarian invaders who crossed the Danube therefore always tended, when they had exhausted the resources of the Balkans, to move westward and add to the embarrassments of the West. . . . The greater part of the Eastern Empire—Asia Minor, Syria, and Egypt—was more or less immune from invasion, and provided the resources to maintain the imperial armies in the Balkans, which, though frequently invaded, were regularly recovered from the impregnable bridgehead of Constantinople.[28]

Last, easy money permits core elites to fight wars, resist liberation struggles, and finance bloated core states.

3. Predicting which, if any, of these factors will intervene to prevent decline or retard attrition and when is impossible. The logic of decay militates against the persistence or creation of exceptionally strong, hypercentralized core states. Because empires are by definition great powers with, presumably, a host of adversaries, we do not as a rule expect them to be courted or coddled by their neighbors, especially in periods of decline. As to geography, although empires can be situated in any corner of the globe, we expect them to emerge in the very thick of political and military struggles and not in remote areas. Easy money, finally, is like an asteroid: it either cannot be predicted at all, or if it can—because an empire just happens to be sitting on a vast pool of oil—it cannot be predicted by any theory of empire.

We *can* account for the emergence of these factors historically. We can trace the emergence of Soviet totalitarianism to, say, Communist ideology,

Stalin's personality, the imperatives of late modernization, capitalist encirclement, and so on.[29] Ottoman Turkey's relative geostrategic importance
makes perfect sense in terms of nineteenth-century great-power competition
in general and the "Great Game" in Central Asia in particular.[30] Austria-
Hungary better served Germany's strategic purposes alive than dead.[31] Favorable geographic location is overwhelmingly a function of natural barriers
to invasion, such as mountains, rivers, deserts, and oceans. Vast natural
wealth is the result of geological or other natural developments on the one
hand and economic demand on the other.

Although props, like shocks, are anything but mysterious phenomena, we
cannot say, at time t, that some factor will intervene at $t + n$ to save a
decrepit empire. Geographic location is the only candidate for such status—
after all, rivers, ranges, and oceans do not come and go at the whim of
constructivist scholars—but, even here, we have no way of knowing that
technological means or geopolitical alignments will not render such obstacles irrelevant. Constantinople's location may have saved it from the barbarians in the fifth century; that very same location did not save it from the
Ottomans one thousand years later.

4. All is not lost. Because no intervening variable is permanent by nature,
it can at best only delay attrition. More important, by delaying attrition, these
variables may actually make decaying empires more susceptible to collapse.
I have already suggested how this dynamic could work in the case of hypercentralized states. They keep peripheral elites under control by intensifying
the periphery-to-core resource flow and thereby accelerating decay. But such
a balancing act cannot be sustained for too long. At some future time the
contradictory pressures acting on the core state, and of course on the imperial economy, may prove too strong for it to sustain both enormous state
control and so high a degree of resource extraction. As a result, hypercentralized states should make empires especially susceptible to disintegration,
if and when even relatively minor crises strike.

Alliances—or, more generally, a favorable geopolitical environment—are
no less of a mixed blessing. The decaying empire finds safety in the embrace
of a big brother, but, by the same token, it becomes hostage to his policies
and behavior. Those may be pacific but in all likelihood will be belligerent:
after all, ascendant expansionist powers looking to flex their muscles and
claim a place in the sun should be most inclined to shelter decaying empires.
During World War I, in Kann's words, "the strait jacket of the German
alliance was, of course, one of the most important factors which prevented

the arrangement not only of a separate peace between the [Habsburg] monarchy and the Western Allies but of the arrangement of a general negotiated peace between all the warring parties as well."[32] Worse, the alliance may embolden the big brother to be even more aggressive toward other states. It can also incline the core elite of the decaying empire to be less cautious, on the ground that its oversized sibling can always save it from policy mistakes.[33] Just such a calculation appears to have figured in the decision of Habsburg elites to go to war against Serbia in July 1914, when a "set of leaders experienced in statecraft, power and crisis management consciously risked a general war to fight a local war."[34]

Easy money is also a two-edged sword. By saving the empire from decline and encouraging the state to intensify its control of the periphery precisely as the forces of decay are eating away at the empire's foundations, easy money makes the empire especially vulnerable to capricious future disruptions in the flow of resources or fluctuations in prices.[35] The 1978 revolution in Iran, for instance, was at least partly the result of the drop in oil revenues that occurred just before.[36] Silver and gold from the New World sustained Spain, but once prices dropped because of overproduction, so too did the empire's fortunes.[37] Siberian oil and gas propped up the Soviet regime in the 1980s, but with world overproduction and concomitant price reductions, natural resources could not sustain imperial rule past the short term.[38] More important, because easy money is the product of the sudden acquisition of seemingly limitless wealth, it necessarily loses value over time, as the more there is of it—whether oil, silver, gold, or timber—the less it is worth, as prices fall and revenues decline.

A favorable geographic location may most resemble an unconditional asset. Geographic isolation of the kind enjoyed by, say, the United States is a fact of nature, whereas mere distance from great-power contests, of the kind enjoyed by Romanov Russia, is a relative asset that, like the Maginot Line, cannot keep war and conflict permanently away. But even a favorable location can redound to an empire's disadvantage. The strategic value of marginality or isolation may be obvious, but the economic costs can more than offset it. Economic isolation may reduce an empire's access to capital, technology, and trade and in the long run retard its development and diminish its capacity to compete internationally. Bernard Lewis, for instance, attributes the long-term decline of the Ottoman Empire to the discovery of the New World and the resultant shift of economic activity from the eastern Mediterranean to the Atlantic.[39] Similarly, Henri Pirenne famously argued that the Muslim conquest of the Mediterranean transposed the cultural and political center of Europe from the south to the north.[40]

Shocks

Whereas attrition is premised on informality of rule, sustained resource diversions, and state decline, collapse is not. Because the peripheries of decayed empires are, ipso facto, more autonomous than they were before decay set in, they have, at least in principle, the capacity to act as more or less full-fledged states. Not so the peripheries of collapsed empires. Some may have been the beneficiaries of decay; others may have been the objects of formal rule and core-state intrusiveness. As the rapid and comprehensive dismantling of the hublike structure of empire, collapse therefore produces "free-floating" peripheries and a core. The spokes of the rimless wheel, P-C-P, disappear, but the P-C-P relationship need not be replaced by P-P-P, Z-P-Z, or P-Z-P relationships.

The P-C-P relationship can break down completely and collapse only if the core is destroyed or temporarily debilitated. Either way, some sort of shock appears to be necessary. A sudden change in climate may have destroyed the Akkadian empire; world war brought down the Habsburg, Romanov, Ottoman, and Wilhelmine empires; the Aztecs proved powerless against the intrusion of diseases brought to their shores by hopelessly outnumbered conquistadores.[41] Indeed, the arrival of Cortés in 1519 was quintessentially exogenous to developments in Mesoamerica. Although Moctezuma II ruled at the high point of Aztec expansion, he was easily defeated by a few hundred men who produced what Geoffrey Conrad and Arthur Demarest call a "Spanish holocaust."[42]

Brian Fagan's systematic investigation of the effect of natural catastrophes on polities reinforces the theoretical importance of shocks: "There are only a limited number of ways societies can respond to accumulated climatic stress: movement or social collaboration; muddling their way from crisis to crisis; decisive, centralized leadership on the part of a few individuals; or developing innovations that increase the carrying capacity of the land. The alternative to all these options is collapse."[43] Although collapse may therefore not be inevitable in principle, it may be inevitable in reality if for some reason societies are incapable of responding in one of Fagan's prescribed ways.

Although natural scientists know much about the causes and consequences of disease, climate shifts, and other destabilizing natural phenomena, and although social scientists also have some authoritative statements
to make about comparable social phenomena, their collective wisdom is of
little relevance to a theory of imperial decline. Such a theory perforce has
little to say about plagues, hurricanes, asteroids, and man-made cataclysms,
except to acknowledge that they can affect political systems and that, because
they occur for reasons extrinsic to the theory, they are necessarily unpredictable. Why system-shattering shocks emerge and where they come from
are questions that theories of revolution may be able to answer but that
theories of empire—and especially a structural theory of empire—cannot.
All such a theory can do is invoke the ultimately unpredictable nature of
much of reality and point to chaos theory, Heisenberg's uncertainty principle, Gödel's theorem, and the like for moral support.[44] (Somewhat more
encouragingly, Ehrhard Behrens suggests that some mathematical problems
can be solved only through chance![45]) Negative evidence for the validity of
this proposition is found in James Rosenau's study of "turbulence," which
attempts to explain "high complexity and dynamism" in terms of an analytical framework that combines macro with micro perspectives and a whole
host of actors, ranging from states to individuals, and amounts to a theory of
everything.[46]

This is not to say that shocks are convenient dei ex machinis and that
there is absolutely nothing to be said about the probability of their occur-
rence. Although it may be impossible to predict earthquakes with accuracy,
geologists do know that they are far more likely to occur in certain places
than in others. "El Niño," writes Fagan, "is a chaotic pendulum, with pro-
tean mood swings that can last months, decades, even centuries or millennia.
The pendulum never follows exactly the same path, for even minor variations in wind patterns can cause dramatic changes down the line. But there
is an underlying rhythm to the swings, like a set of musical variations endlessly circling a central theme."[47] In similar fashion Joseph Tainter notes:

> As the marginal return on complexity declines, complexity as a strategy
> yields comparatively lower benefits at higher and higher costs. A so-
> ciety that cannot counter this trend, such as through acquisition of an
> energy subsidy, becomes vulnerable to stress surges that it is too weak
> or impoverished to meet, and to waning support in its population.
> With continuation of this trend collapse becomes a matter of mathe-

matical probability, as over time an insurmountable stress surge becomes increasingly likely. Until such a challenge occurs, there may be a period of economic stagnation, political decline, and territorial shrinkage.[48]

Humanly contrived shocks may be equally unpredictable in this sense without, as a result, being utterly random and inexplicable events. Several generalizations are thus possible and useful:

1. Shocks can be grouped into the following broad categories: natural phenomena, such as droughts, plagues, asteroids, earthquakes, and the like; wars, invasions, and other kinds of military conflicts; socioeconomic developments, such as mass migrations and economic depressions; and political changes, such as the death of a charismatic leader, misguided reform efforts, revolutions, and so on.

Natural phenomena are, as noted, completely beyond the grasp of any theory of empire. Military conflicts may be considered a constant, part of the international background against which all imperial trajectories are played out. Socioeconomic developments are no less a permanent part of the internal development of all states. Political change is also a constant, although one that is likely to occur most often in decaying and malfunctioning empires ripe for revolution, rebellion, transformation, and the like. In a word, only the first category, natural phenomena, is truly exogenous, while the latter three can fit into the interstices of a theory of imperial decline, and political change arguably can be made a function of imperial decay. Theda Skocpol's theory of revolution could, when seen in this light, be easily translated into imperial terms. She attributes the inability of agrarian autocracies to modernize to their class structure. We can agree, while adding that this structure was both resilient and obstructive precisely because peripheral class elites enjoyed the administrative autonomy inherent in every severely decayed imperial structure.[49]

2. Ceteris paribus, we expect different types of shocks to affect empires differently along various points of the parabola. Natural phenomena are likely to be most devastating during periods of ascendance or decline and not at times of systemic stability. Wars will be most destructive the further along the parabola an empire is located. We expect ascendant empires to win most wars and decaying empires to lose most.[50] Socioeconomic shocks should devastate decaying empires most, ascendant empires less, and stable empires least. The death of a leader, misguided reforms, and other internal

developments will affect decaying and ascendant empires most and stable, well-functioning, institutionalized empires least. Alexander the Great's untimely demise, which, according to A. B. Bosworth, "led inevitably to the dismemberment of his empire," is a case in point.[51]

3. What qualifies as a shock with respect to one system may not with respect to another. Sick systems, like sick patients, can die from colds; healthy systems, like healthy patients, generally do not. The more vigorous the empire, the more cataclysmic the shocks must be to push it into oblivion. The more decrepit the empire, the more run-of-the-mill the shock, the more it can approximate a mere problem. Clearly, problems are legion, perhaps even infinite in number. Real cataclysms, however we define the modifier, are far smaller in kind and in number.

4. It follows that the number of events qualifying as potential shocks increases with the degree of imperial decay. We know by analogy that feeble people are more likely to suffer illnesses, accidents, and the like, both because their immune systems are weakened and because the remedies they take are more likely to have adverse effects.[52] As a result, although the rapid and comprehensive dismantling of an empire can occur anywhere along the parabola, we expect it to strike most often along the downward slope.

5. It also follows that, because empires experience decay unevenly, shocks should affect different parts of an empire differently. Major shocks, or cataclysms, should destroy any weakened system, especially if the advanced decay is spread evenly. When shocks are minor, however, we expect them to affect differentially decayed empires differently. Evenly decayed empires should be more prone to disintegrate rapidly and comprehensively than unevenly decayed empires, which, we surmise, should be more inclined to lose only those chunks of territory that are most autonomous. As we shall see in chapter 4, the evenness of decay can significantly affect the likelihood that empire will be revived in the aftermath of collapse.

6. Because the pool of potential shocks expands with the degree of decay, the probability that cataclysms will bring about collapse becomes correspondingly smaller than the probability that mere problems will do the trick. Asteroids can still strike, of course, but we expect decaying empires to be more likely to collapse for noncataclysmic reasons. The barbarian invasions that contributed to the downfalls of Han China and Rome, for instance, were little different from similar such incursions in both empires' past. What mattered was their internal weakness, their inability to withstand and cope with shocks that they once easily survived.

7. Although we cannot account for the functional equivalent of asteroids, earthquakes, plagues, or climactic shifts, it may be possible to do so for some portion of the vast number of potential shocks that could affect a particular class of decaying systems—those whose attrition has been arrested. When decaying empires should undergo attrition but do not, collapse is likely to be the result of shocks that directly affect the factors that arrest the downward trajectory.

Collapsing Empires

A look at the causes of the collapse of Romanov Russia, Wilhelmine Germany, Austria-Hungary, Ottoman Turkey, and the USSR will help us refine some of these points. The Russian Empire was drawn into and devastated by World War I; the Reich lost a two-front war. In contrast, the Ottoman realm collapsed after substantially less destructive warfare, Habsburg territories were never invaded, and the Soviet Union was not even implicated in a major war at the time of collapse (its foray into Afghanistan, however bloody and demoralizing, does not qualify). And yet, all five empires collapsed, disappearing in the course of several years, as in the Soviet and Ottoman cases, or of one year, as with Romanov Russia and Wilhelmine Germany, or, even, of a few weeks, as was the case with the Habsburg realm. Because the Romanovs and Hohenzollerns suffered defeat or devastation or both, their collapse makes sense. As the Habsburgs, Ottomans, and Soviets suffered neither of these misfortunes, their collapse is puzzling. As we shall see, the shocks that brought down these three empires undermined the props that kept them in a state of suspended attrition.

World War I directly undermined the tsarist imperial state in two ways. First, and most obviously, world war destroyed Russia. Its army was no match for Germany's, and the Russian economy began to unravel under the pressures of mass mobilization and near-total war.[53] In February 1917 a new regime replaced tsarism in Petrograd, but the empire itself began dissolving soon after the authority of the provisional government declined precipitously under conditions of chaos in Russian cities and villages. The Bolshevik coup d'état was also the coup de grace for the empire. Borderland elites who had heretofore strived only for autonomy interpreted the Bolshevik seizure of power as an illegitimate usurpation and the de facto end of empire. The German advance, the initial inability of the Bolsheviks to extend their power far beyond the Petrograd-Moscow axis, and the subsequent civil war between Reds and Whites provided additional opportunities for the borderlands to strike out on their own.[54] By the middle of 1918 most non-Russian elites had declared independence, a condition they were to enjoy until 1920–1921, when, with the exception of Finland, Poland, Estonia, Latvia, and Lithuania, they fell to the onslaughts of the Red Army.[55]

Second, and no less catastrophic for Russia's imperial system, World War I directly undermined the protected status the empire had enjoyed on the geographic margins of the European state system. Unlike other states embroiled in incessant conflicts on all fronts since the Middle Ages, Muscovy remained relatively sheltered from such rivalries.[56] On the one hand, thanks to geography it was far removed from the center of great-power conflicts — a fact that contributed to the undoing of Charles XII of Sweden and of Napoleon; on the other hand, declining Poland served as a buffer between Russia and ascendant Prussia. Poland's disappearance in the late eighteenth century and Germany's emergence as a great power in the late nineteenth exposed Russia to attrition from the West, but it was World War I that drew Russia into an all-European conflict, exposed it to superior military forces, resulted in foreign occupation of provinces that had experienced the greatest decay, and destroyed the imperial state's capacity to retain control of its rebellious peripheries.

Unlike Russia, Wilhelmine Germany was at the height of its power when World War I broke out.[57] Economic growth had been especially impressive, involving a 25 percent increase in gross national product between 1908 and 1913, based in large part on considerable advances in coal, iron, and electricity production and in the chemicals and motor industries.[58] Even so, the Reich quickly lost most of its overseas colonies: Togo, New Guinea, and Tsingtao in late 1914, South-West Africa in 1915, and Cameroon in 1916. Although Germany's wartime efforts were prodigious, victory in Europe may have become impossible after the entry into the war of the United States, which tipped the balance economically against the Reich. As Austria-Hungary proved to be an unreliable ally in the east, Germany had to hold the front in Russia and Ukraine while simultaneously coping with Britain, France, and the United States in the west. The strain on Germany's resources was too great, and in late 1918 it could no longer sustain the war effort.[59] German forces broke rank, while revolutionary disturbances at home replaced imperial rule with a democratic regime. The front collapsed in the chaos that followed, and German forces retreated from the recently occupied territories in east and west. German troops in East Africa also surrendered. Defeated and weakened, the Reich formally lost its holdings after hostilities had ceased, when the terms of the peace deprived it of territories in Africa, the Pacific, and parts of Europe.[60]

Austria was widely acknowledged to be a declining power by all its neighbors since the middle of the nineteenth century. Nevertheless, the imperatives of balance-of-power politics demanded that the territory under Vienna's rule remain Habsburg, lest a dangerous power vacuum emerge in the center of Europe. A striking illustration of Austria's position was Bismarck's decision after Sadowa not to march on Vienna and to leave the Habsburg realm more or less intact.[61] Seen in this light, the Austro-German alliance of 1879 merely ratified Austria-Hungary's peculiar geopolitical position in general and its importance to Wilhelmine Germany in particular. With German power as the guarantor of Habsburg integrity, Austria-Hungary received a lease on life. By the same token, Germany's defeat in war precipitated Austria-Hungary's collapse.[62] Enervated by the war and deprived of its protector, a highly decayed imperial system fell apart into regions and elites for the most part already beyond Vienna's control.

Unlike Austria-Hungary, the Ottoman Empire had experienced significant attrition in the course of the nineteenth century; like Austria-Hungary, it collapsed only after World War I. The war overtaxed the empire's backward economy and military, but because the Ottoman realm was spared the brute devastation of Romanov Russia, some other factor must have precipitated collapse. The Ottoman Empire, not unlike Austria-Hungary, lived on as the sick man of Europe because of a geopolitical environment that favored its continued survival. World War I destroyed that environment; more important, it undermined the Central Powers, which directly supported Constantinople. Only after Germany lost and Austria-Hungary fell apart were the Ottomans, under pressure from nationalist forces commanded by Mustafa Kemal, no longer able to continue as an imperial house and as a realm.[63]

The Soviet empire could weather decay precisely because the party-state was totalitarian, maintaining an elaborate system of recruitment and control that sustained its rule even after decay had assumed alarming proportions in the 1970s and 1980s.[64] Totalitarianism kept the peripheries bound to the core, despite the terrible economic price it exacted. Indeed, by the end of Leonid Brezhnev's reign decay had accelerated to the point where totalitarianism could no longer reproduce and sustain itself.[65] Mikhail Gorbachev's reforms were supposed to save the system, but instead perestroika destroyed the empire. Reneo Lukic and Allen Lynch provide a good account of the cataclysmic effect of Gorbachev's policies:

> In the face of the post-Stalinist legacy of increased real power in the hands of the national communist leaders of the union republics, and by his insistence on making the central Communist Party the primary agency of structural reform, Gorbachev ensured both the demise of the supranational Soviet Communist Party . . . and the establishment of nationally based political movements and institutions as the sole alternative to Soviet communism, reform or otherwise. In seeking to transform a Communist Party whose large majority was uncomprehending if not unsympathetic or even hostile to his reform enterprise, Gorbachev ensured the neutralization of the only political institution in the Soviet Union with a supranational vocation. At the same time, by seeking to contain reformist forces under the umbrella of the putatively reformed central Communist Party, while also tolerating and even encouraging a degree of political latitude unprecedented in Soviet history, Gorbachev lost whatever chances might have existed for establishing a supranational alternative to the Soviet Communist Party.[66]

By targeting the party at a time of advanced decay and national communist mobilization, Gorbachev's reforms subverted its organizational overlordship in east-central Europe and the republics.[67] As a result, according to Valerie Bunce, "the tightly integrated structure of the bloc also meant that changes in the Soviet Union, whether in policy or personnel, tended to spread rapidly to Eastern Europe—whether the Soviets wanted that to happen or not and, quite often, in a form and level of intensity that the Soviets neither expected nor welcomed. The bloc structure, therefore, tended to *magnify* Soviet developments as they traveled westward."[68] Once totalitarianism was dismantled, the imperial rule that was premised on totalitarian control began to dissolve.

My argument demotes Gorbachev from the potential status of a hero in history to a well-meaning, if hapless leader who stumbled into the USSR's collapse. Some scholars would disagree with this characterization—Archie Brown, for instance[69]—but it surely is true that Gorbachev never intended to destroy the Soviet Union, and it is also the case that he had scant appreciation of the explosive nature of the Soviet nationality question.[70] Seen in this light, Gorbachev closely resembles the erratic Nikita Khrushchev: both leaders attempted to address the inefficiencies identified by Karl Deutsch in a manner that, while laudable perhaps, was profoundly destabilizing. The major difference therefore consists not in the leader but in the condition of the system. In the late 1950s and early 1960s the Soviet empire was vigorous and powerful. By the mid-1980s it had just emerged from the "era of stagnation."[71] Under conditions such as these, reform of any kind was probably lethal.

In sum, Russia was struck by a cataclysm that was both enormously destructive and subversive of its geographic isolation. Its collapse was overdetermined. Germany lost a war that left it, relatively speaking, more or less unscathed but completely vulnerable to the punitive policies of the victors, who stripped it of its colonies. Austria-Hungary's alliance with Germany meant that German defeat would result in Habsburg collapse. War weakened the Ottoman Empire, while its alignment with the losers deprived it of the geopolitical solicitude of the defeated Central Powers on the one hand and the triumphant Triple Entente on the other. Finally, perestroika devastated the hypercentralized totalitarian state and thereby undermined the Soviet empire.

Variations

In discussing these factors, I have assumed that they prop up empires uniformly. We know, of course, that some parts of an empire will be more isolated than others, that easy money will not flow evenly, that geopolitical environments can be more or less favorable to different parts of an empire, and, most important perhaps, that hypercentralized rule will not be evenly distributed. As a result, just as uneven decay can contribute to different outcomes, so too the uneven effect of sustaining factors can produce different results.

Consider the dissimilar ways in which Austria-Hungary, Romanov Russia, and the USSR collapsed. The Habsburg realm was more or less evenly decayed, and its alliance with Germany had no differential effect on Habsburg territories. As a result, the dismantling of the imperial relationship occurred virtually over night, in early November 1918. The Germans, Czechs, and Slovaks founded republics, Hungarians became embroiled in a civil war, South Slavs established a state, and Poles and Ukrainians fought over Galicia. The degree of turmoil varied from region to region, and more or less stable states emerged only in 1919–1920, but the rapid and comprehensive disappearance of Habsburg authority over the peripheries was indisputable.[72]

In Romanov Russia, in contrast, those parts of the empire that had enjoyed greatest autonomy as imperial peripheries, had been occupied longest by German or Austrian troops, and had been spared the ravages of the most destructive trench warfare were most likely to separate and to do so successfully. The geography of imperial decay thus combined with the geography of war to produce a process of collapse that affected different parts of the empire differently. Finland had possessed a variety of protostate institutions, including its own parliament and constitution, even in Romanov times; during the war it managed to avoid reoccupation by virtue of its geographic location. The Baltic states, which should not by any measure have been able to stand up to the Red Army, had the good fortune of possessing indigenous protopolitical institutions developed by Baltic German elites, of being occupied by the German army, and of being located far from the central arena of the civil war in the southeast. Poland, finally, retained its political, cultural, and social elites throughout the nineteenth century, and, thanks to German rule, was able to acquire and nurture its independence during the war. In stark contrast, such minimally decayed regions as Ukraine and Belarus also had the misfortune of being devastated by the front, while the informally ruled khanates of Khiva and Bukhara had nowhere to go and thus could fall prey to Bolshevik predations.[73]

The Soviet empire experienced both uneven decay—with east-central Europe the most decayed and the non-Russian republics the least decayed— as well as uneven totalitarian rule, with east-central Europe the least afflicted and the non-Russian republics the most afflicted. As we would expect, the east-central Europeans acquired independence in 1989, in no small measure thanks to their own national revolts, while the non-Russian republics had to wait until the USSR itself collapsed in late 1991. All the east-central Europeans had enjoyed semiautonomous satellite status since at least the 1960s, with Poland, Hungary, Yugoslavia, and to a lesser extent Czechoslovakia actually developing substantial elements of state capacity, civil society, market economies, and rule of law.[74]

The non-Russian republics were also unevenly decayed. The Baltic states had enjoyed substantial autonomy since the 1960s, when they began serving as laboratories for social, economic, and political experiments usually involving devolutions of authority. Moreover, by virtue of having been incorporated into the USSR only after World War II, they managed to enjoy twenty years of independence and escape the worst of Stalinist terror.[75] Not surprisingly, the Balts led the drive for national liberation and, after 1991, were in the forefront of political and economic reform. In stark contrast, the Central Asian republics enjoyed the least autonomy within the Soviet Union and proved to be most reluctant to pursue independence and, after independence, to pursue reform. Such middle-of-the-road Soviet republics as Ukraine, Moldova, and the three Caucasus states were in general less independence-minded than the Balts and east-central Europeans and more independence-minded than the Central Asians.[76]

After Collapse

Unlike attrition, which ineluctably deimperializes an empire by reducing it to a shell of its former self, collapse need not result in the end of empire. We know that empirically, but we can also deduce this from a closer look at how collapse affects empire. After all, collapse ensues if and when the core is weakened and cannot play the role of a hub. Shocks can so rattle a system as to produce a breakdown in the interactions between and among its parts. As the imperial spokes "disappear," the peripheries are left on their own as formally independent polities. But formal independence does not necessarily mean the disappearance of empire as a system. "The boundaries of social systems," writes Raimondo Strassoldo, "are not only spatial, but also functional; a social system is said to exist as long as its components display certain behaviours, states, and attributes. At the moment its variations exceed certain critical values or norms, the system is said to be stressed, disintegrated or to have become something else."[77] Because the shocks that produce collapse can be of various types—ranging from cataclysms to mere problems— and because the empires struck by shocks can be positioned at various points of Taagepera's parabolas, we have no reason to think that the "behaviors, states, and attributes" of the core and periphery have necessarily become transformed and that the breakdown of the *P-C-P* relationship is therefore permanent. We know that a shock may result in collapse, or it may not. In turn, collapse may—but need not—result in nonexistence. The imperial system, like a patient in a critical condition, may revive.[78]

4 Imperial Revival

A structural theory cannot predict which collapsed empires will revive; it can only point to the structural conditions that make revival possible and likely. In so doing, the theory need not go beyond its domain and thereby flirt with theorizing everything. Collapse comes about from the chance intervention of shocks that push a system, however vigorous or decayed, over the edge. Revival, in contrast, is not serendipitous: it can occur only if the empire that collapsed possessed certain characteristics when the shock struck. As a result, revival is not just a return to the status quo ante. In a very real sense, revival is the continuation of the status quo ante: revival is what *would* have happened if shocks had not intervened. As we know, such a counterfactual conditional can hold only if a theory underpins it. That theory is, for better or for worse, the theory of decline presented in this book.

As I argue in this chapter, a relatively strong core state constitutes a necessary condition of revival, and the evenness of decay and the degree of continuity are its facilitating conditions. Thus revival is impossible if decay is advanced or if, even with minimal decay, the postcollapse core state is weak. Alternatively, if and when revival is possible, it is more likely to occur if decay is even and territorial continuity is substantial. Although my discussion of the aftermath of collapse in the Habsburg, Ottoman, Romanov, Wilhelmine, and Soviet contexts will, naturally enough, corroborate my theoretical expectations—this is, after all, the final chapter and provocative conclusions are de rigeur—I emphasize that the appearance of inevitability is stylistic and not causal.

Conditions of Revival

In the absence of significant decay, and, as always, ceteris paribus, we expect the former core to possess a full-fledged state comprising an experienced state elite, a coherent bureaucratic apparatus, and a functioning army and police force. We also expect all peripheral entities at best only to approximate states. As imperial outposts they necessarily lack the organizations that constitute fully developed Weberian states, possessing only emasculated elites, incoherent collections of administrators, and, perhaps, directionless forces of coercion. Under conditions of advanced decay, core states will be substantially weaker, whereas peripheral entities will more closely approximate actual polities.[1] In a minimally decayed empire, therefore, a former core possesses greater "state capacity" than its former peripheries; in empires suffering from advanced decay, state capacity will be more evenly balanced between core and periphery.[2] Because revival is premised on the former core state's ability to dominate the former periphery, minimal decay, or its equivalent, is, for obvious reasons, a prerequisite of revival.[3]

That equivalent is the relative capacity of the core state. Decay may be advanced and former peripheries may possess substantial state capacity, but a former core, if it is especially large and resource rich, can still confront the peripheries with formidable political challenges.[4] It is impossible to say how large and powerful the core will be at the point of collapse, but there is no reason that, compared to the periphery, some cores cannot be tiny, others relatively small, and still others huge. Other things being equal, the larger and more resource endowed the former core, the greater its ability to project power and to dominate the former periphery. A powerful core is therefore the functional equivalent of minimal decay.

These fairly straightforward realist observations, when combined with my comments regarding extent of decay, suggest that postimperial core-periphery relations can, ceteris paribus, be structured in these ways:

    I. A powerful core with poorly endowed peripheries
    II. A powerful core with well-endowed peripheries
    III. A weak core with well-endowed peripheries
    IV. A weak core with poorly endowed peripheries

A powerful core and poorly endowed peripheries (I) are almost certain to be implicated in a reconstituted imperial relationship. We expect the former core to dominate the former peripheries, the former peripheries to continue to be dependent on the former core, and the chances of the former peripheries' joining together to balance against the core or even to cooperate with one another to be small. With all these structural forces in place, the complete reestablishment of empire is highly probable. Empire is also possible if a powerful core confronts well-endowed peripheries (II), but we have no way to determine the degree of possibility. Depending on how powerful the core is and how advanced decay was, we can imagine a range of outcomes, from the core's dominating the periphery to both sides' being involved in continual tugging and pulling to their coexisting in the form of a commonwealth. The remaining two combinations preclude revival. A weak core and well-endowed peripheries (III) will probably coexist as independent states. A weak core and poorly endowed peripheries (IV) should drift apart, with the former retaining its independence and the latter perhaps falling under the hegemonic sway of other powers.

Although empire is most likely to reemerge in full bloom when a powerful core looms above poorly endowed peripheries (I), the possibility of imperial revival will be enhanced when a powerful core faces well-endowed peripheries (II) under two conditions—the decay is uneven and the empire is territorially continuous.

Because some peripheries will be more decayed than others in unevenly decayed empires, we expect informally ruled peripheries to have greater state capacity than formally ruled ones. We also expect the former to be the beneficiaries of greater economic development, information aggregation, and resource accumulation. In sum, just as we expect less decayed empires to be more likely to revive than more decayed empires, so too we expect the less decayed parts of unevenly decaying empires to be more likely to be brought back into the fold than the more decayed parts.

Territorial continuity, and especially contiguity, is another facilitating condition of both partial and complete revival. Postimperial borders are likely to be administrative demarcations and not real boundaries marking off one territory and one set of political and economic institutions from others. As a result, a more or less seamless web of institutions should continue to span borders.[5] As the core will have penetrated the periphery with its institutions in imperial times, we expect the core's economic activities, social norms, and political practices to have disseminated and perhaps taken root. Peripheral institutions and conventions may also have made some headway into the core. Institutional penetration and interpenetration translate into an intermingling of populations, at least along the administrative border between core and periphery, with inhabitants of the periphery likely to settle in the core and inhabitants of the core likely to settle in the periphery, where they can serve as agents of the empire as well.[6]

Different combinations of the extent and evenness of decay will, if core power is held constant (i.e., large), also have a differential effect on the likelihood of imperial reconstitution. Thus evenly distributed advanced decay precludes the possibility of imperial revival. Evenly distributed minimal decay facilitates complete revival, whereas unevenly distributed advanced decay should permit the revival of imperial relations between the former core and those parts that were least decayed. Finally, unevenly distributed minimal decay should make partial reconstitution likely. If the empire is continuous, we expect partial revival to be even "more possible" under conditions of unevenly distributed advanced decay and "more likely" under conditions of unevenly distributed minimal decay. If the empire is discontinuous, we expect partial revival to be "less possible" under conditions of evenly distributed advanced decay and "less likely" under conditions of evenly distributed minimal decay.

If all four factors—extent of decay, evenness of decay, relative core power, and continuity—are present in just the right way, postcollapse relations between territorially contiguous former peripheries and their former core almost perfectly approximate the conditions under which a strong metropole, a vulnerable periphery, transnational forces, and a facilitating international environment interact in Michael Doyle's scheme to produce imperial penetration of the periphery by the metropole.[7] We therefore expect the probability of complete imperial revival to be high when decay is minimal and evenly distributed at the time of collapse, the relative power of the core state is great, and the empire is territorially continuous. Complete revival—indeed, revival of any kind—should be less or least probable when decay is high and evenly distributed and when the relative power of the core state and continuity are small.

Naturally, any number of intermediate outcomes can also be constructed. Thus a low level of decay in just two of N peripheries bordering on the core, in combination with large relative core power, should facilitate the emergence of at least part of the former empire. In contrast, a high level of decay in a contiguous empire on the one hand and a still-powerful core on the other may or may not result in empire—the outcome is indeterminate and contingent—but it is likely to produce unstable relations between the former core and the former peripheries, as they jostle for definition in highly uncertain circumstances.

Reimperialization

How do our case studies stack up against these expectations? The next section briefly illustrates how the four factors affected post-Habsburg Austria, post-Ottoman Turkey, post-Romanov Russia, and post-Wilhelmine Germany—leading to, respectively, no imperial revival in the first and second cases, substantial revival in the third, and instability and attempted revival in the fourth. Although the fit is not perfect, it is sufficiently close to support the theory and warrant applying it to post-Soviet circumstances.

The Habsburg and Ottoman Empires

The extent of decay varied for most of Habsburg history but in general was greatest in Hungary, Croatia-Slavonia, and Lombardy, and smallest in Bohemia, Moravia, and Galicia. The *Ausgleich* of 1867 institutionalized decay by granting Hungary something in the nature of satellite status vis-à-vis Austria. Soon thereafter Czech nationalists claimed autonomy for Bohemia, the Polish nobility strengthened its hold on Galicia, and the empire became increasingly less formal even within Cisleithania.[8] As a result, decay was both advanced and fairly even when World War I broke out. Finally, the empire had been highly continuous since the late 1860s, by which time outlying territories in Belgium, Germany, and Italy had succumbed to attrition.

Decay afflicted the Ottoman Empire in similar fashion. Ottoman power reached its height in the seventeenth century. Thereafter the drift toward decay and informal rule began, resulting in substantial attrition in the nineteenth century, when various territories acquired independence—Egypt under Muhammad Ali was the most significant instance—or, like Tunisia, Libya, and the Dodecanese Islands, were lost to other states. The territories that remained Ottoman—such as Lebanon, Syria, Serbia, Montenegro, and the Romanian principalities—increasingly became the bailiwicks of peripheral elites.[9] The empire was also discontinuous, with peripheries located far from the core, at distances that were reinforced by natural barriers, such as deserts, mountains, and large bodies of water.

Situated on the downward slope of the parabola at the time of collapse in 1918, the Habsburg and Ottoman realms bequeathed comparatively low levels of state capacity to Austria and Turkey. In the former, decay had advanced to such an extent that, after the *Ausgleich*, Hungary was for all practical purposes a second core. In the decades that followed 1867, Bohemia and Moravia not only acquired extensive political rights but also became the driving force of the empire's economic development. In 1918, therefore, Austria, Hungary, and Czechoslovakia stood on more or less equal terms as ministates with more or less equal endowments of resources.[10] Kemalist Turkey was more robust as a state, having asserted its sovereignty in the face of military interventions by the Triple Entente and Greece. However, Turkish elites could do little to rectify the interwar geopolitical imbalance that had emerged in response to the regional instability in their neighborhood. To the south were territories under British and French mandates; to the north and east was the Soviet Union; to the west were states that had emerged from successful liberation struggles against the Ottomans in the nineteenth and twentieth centuries.[11]

The Russian Empire

Imperial Russian rule varied; generally, it was or became most formal in territories acquired in the seventeenth and eighteenth centuries (Kazan', Astrakhan, Belorussia, and Little Russia) and most informal in such later acquisitions as Poland, Finland, Transcaucasia, Bukhara, and Khiva — where local nobles, emirs, and khans served as peripheral elites.[12] Like the Habsburg empire, the Romanov realm decayed, but, unlike the Habsburg empire, decay in late imperial Russia varied both in terms of breadth and depth. The empire was also highly discontinuous, with significant chunks bordering on the core and just as many peripheries distant therefrom.

Compared to the non-Russian protostates that declared independence in 1918–1919, Bolshevik Russia, which housed the empire's urban and industrial base, possessed impressive armed forces, elites, and resources.[13] Small wonder that the Bolsheviks could easily defeat most of the non-Russian nationalists in the course of 1918–1921. As I noted in chapter 3, where external intervention by Germany or Austria-Hungary abetted internal state building on the one hand and where the devastation of the front by-passed peripheries on the other, the non-Russians could and generally did succeed in claiming independence. Where such fortuitous circumstances did not intervene, non-Russian states fell to the Bolsheviks with relative ease.[14]

The German Empire

Decay in the German Reich was minimal, perhaps even nonexistent. Germany had emerged as a unified empire only in 1871. In the four decades that followed, it had experienced impressive industrial and military growth, consolidating its state capacity, establishing firm control over its Slavic borderlands, and extending imperial rule into Africa and the Pacific. Germany was an empire in ascendance, not in decline.[15] But it was also both highly continuous, possessing territories in Mitteleuropa, as well as highly discontinuous, with several overseas colonies.

As an ascendant empire, the Reich bequeathed substantial state power to interwar Germany. World War I deprived it of Cameroon, Togo, South-West Africa, East Africa, New Guinea, Tsingtao, Alsace-Lorraine, and parts of Prussia and Poland, but it left the core state and its efficient agencies intact. Moreover, despite onerous reparations and postwar hyperinflation, the economic base remained strong; Germany had been Europe's economic powerhouse before the war and had experienced little actual destruction. Only the military had been reduced to a shell of its former self. As Andreas Hillgruber puts it, "Despite the severity of its defeat in 1918, Germany remained the strongest power in central Europe in economic—and potentially in military—terms. With hindsight, it seems obvious that the German state had the opportunity to regain the hegemonic position it had lost in the First World War."[16] Although the state capacity of interwar Germany was thus generally high, that of many of Germany's neighbors was, individually and collectively, comparable and with respect to military affairs probably superior.[17] France and England remained imperial powers, Poland and Czechoslovakia could capitalize on their relative autonomy within tsarist Russia and Austria-Hungary to build effective states, and the totalitarian Soviet Union was able to mobilize vast resources.[18]

As table 4.1 shows, the four empires fit, *more rather than less*, the pattern described earlier. I had claimed that the probability of revival will be highest if the extent of decay is low and the evenness of decay, core power, and

TABLE 4.1 Probability of Revival

	Habsburg	Ottoman	Romanov	Wilhelmine
Extent of decay	High	High	Medium	Low
Evenness of decay	High	High	Low	High
Power of core	Low	Low	High	Medium
Continuity	High	Low	Medium	Medium

territorial continuity are all high. The probability of revival will be least if the extent and evenness of decay are great and both core power and continuity are low. Of course, where peripheries are the beneficiaries of advanced and even decay, and the former core is not a great power, the empire does not revive, even with respect to peripheries located just across postimperial borders. Post–World War I Austria and Turkey could not, by this logic, have expanded, because a necessary condition of empire, an imbalance of state power, was absent. In contrast, post–World War I Russia enjoyed an overwhelming power imbalance with respect to many, but not all, former Romanov territories, and especially those adjacent to it. In such circumstances partial revival was hardly foreordained but highly likely.

Developments in post–Wilhelmine Germany were far more complicated than this shopping list suggests. The role of Adolf Hitler and the rise to and seizure of power by the Nazis are a central part of the story. Moreover, Nazi expansion entailed far more than imperial revival; it was also an obvious instance of imperial expansion.[19] My checklist suggests only that attempted revival, if not expansion, was both possible and likely, given the concatenation of relations within which the former core and former peripheries were involved in the postwar period.[20]

One factor played an especially important role in the arguments of German expansionists and in facilitating revival—continuity. In the postwar configuration of state boundaries, a substantial number of ethnic Germans located in western Poland, Bohemia, Moravia, and Austria—most of whom were products of Habsburg imperial rule and collapse—were transformed, discursively and ideologically, into "beached" diasporas ostensibly in need of immediate rescue via annexation.[21] Although my theoretical scheme has nothing to say about this transformation, it does suggest why it mattered.

These German minorities were located just across the border with Germany. Once they were identified as abandoned brethren, their presence facilitated cross-border ties and cross-border German influence. Konrad Henlein's Sudeten German Party, like the Nazi Party in Austria, is a case in point: both were supported and financed by the NSDAP in Germany and could make the case for *Anschluss* as well as facilitate Nazi penetration of both states.[22]

The implications of this analysis for post-Soviet Russia are obvious. First, Soviet imperial decay was advanced but uneven—high in the east-central European satellites and relatively low in the non-Russian republics. Second, post-Soviet Russia has, despite its many difficulties, retained enormous relative state capacity. And, third, continuity serves to reinforce the porousness of boundaries, the interpenetration of institutions, and the salience of Russian minorities beached in the newly independent post-Soviet states. Because the conditions prevalent in post-Soviet Russia closely resemble those in the post-Romanov and post-Wilhelmine contexts, we have no choice but to expect partial reimperialization in the former Soviet space.[23]

Soviet Decay

Consider, first, the extent and evenness of decay, where decay is a function of the degree of imperial and totalitarian rule (figure 4.1). If we examine Russia and its neighbors in terms of state capacity and resources, the Soviet empire's successor polities fall into four distinct categories. The first group consists of entities that emerged from the USSR's informal empire in east-central Europe. They were least totalitarian and least imperial and, upon attaining independence in 1989, were best equipped to act as genuinely independent states. In general, they possessed more or less complete state apparatuses, bureaucracies, elites, armies, police forces, and courts, relatively coherent economies, as well as a variety of autonomous social institutions, if not quite full-fledged civil societies.[24]

The second, third, and fourth sets consist of the successor polities of the formal empire—the other non-Russian republics, the Baltic states, and the regions of the Russian Soviet Federated Socialist Republic (RSFSR). The non-Russians possessed their own Communist Parties, bureaucratic apparatus, and the accoutrements of symbolic sovereignty, but they failed to inherit an effective state apparatus.[25] Their bureaucracies were shapeless; their ministries were either understaffed or nonexistent; and their policy-making and

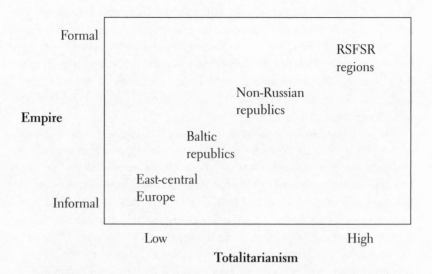

FIGURE 4.1 Post-Soviet Institutional Legacies

policy-implementing cadres, trained to receive orders from Moscow, were anything but effective elites. As I argued in chapter 3, Estonia, Latvia, and Lithuania occupied an intermediate position between the informally ruled east-central Europeans and the formally ruled non-Russians. Finally, the RSFSR had, in Soviet times, been a conglomerate of ethnically organized administrative regions, representing an "inner empire" within the empire. The RSFSR's ethnofederal regions survived collapse and resembled pale copies of the non-Russian successor polities. Like the non-Russian entities, Russia's ethnofederal regions had no state apparatus. But they also had no coherent political elites, having lacked their own Communist Party organizations in Soviet times.[26]

As the core, Russia was in a class of its own. Although it inherited the bulk of the imperial-totalitarian state apparatus and its elites, two Soviet-era deformations afflicted that state. The bureaucracies that staffed central ministries were too large for, and too mismatched with, scaled-down postimperial, post-totalitarian purposes. And the institutions that stood out within the panoply of state agencies inherited from the Soviet period were the still-powerful secret police and army, which were assured a disproportionately influential position in the state by virtue of the comparative weakness of other political institutions.[27] Although they were imposing in Moscow, Russian state agencies had little control over elites and institutions in outlying Russian regions.[28] Totalitarian decay had loosened P-C-P bonds in Brezhnev's times, while imperial collapse had severed them completely. That weakness was compounded by another carryover from imperial times—Russia's ethnofederal structure.[29]

Two additional factors enhanced the relative standing of the ethnofederal regions. First, in a vast country with a poorly developed communications and transportation network, distance effectively sheltered regions from the postimperial state centered in Moscow. Sakha-Yakutia, for instance, is several thousand miles from Moscow. Tatarstan and Bashkortostan are substantially closer in geographic terms but still relatively sheltered by Russia's poor highways, both physical and virtual. The second factor was economic. Although the central state apparatus in Moscow was huge, it was resource poor. It generated few revenues on its own and, as a result of imperial collapse, was hard-pressed to extract resources from the rest of the country. In contrast, many ethnofederal regions were resource rich. Tatarstan had substantial petroleum deposits; Sakha-Yakutia was awash in diamonds and other natural resources; Bashkortostan had oil.[30] Although the ethnofederal regions lacked states, their protoelites had easy money and could embark on state building.

Russian Power

The conventional wisdom has it that Russia is hopelessly weak.[31] Compared to the United States, of course, Russia may be a third-world state with nuclear arms; compared to its neighbors, Russia still is a military superpower and an economic giant.[32] The first war with Chechnya in 1994–1996 seemed to be, as Anatol Lieven put it, the "tombstone of Russian power."[33] The second war that began in 1999 showed that Lieven's judgment was at least premature. More important, regardless of that conflict's denouement, it demonstrated that the Russian military was able to pursue a full-fledged war twice. It may not have done so with the élan that NATO displayed over Kosovo, but it proved that it had the capacity to mobilize soldiers and send them into battle.[34] Russia's neighbors would not, in all likelihood, have been able to engage the Chechens even once. Most have no armies to speak of, and Ukraine—which does have a substantial military—would almost certainly have failed even more miserably than Russia in 1996.[35] Table 4.2, which shows the enormous disparities between Russia's power resources and those of its neighbors in the near abroad, needs no comment.

Table 4.3, meanwhile, illustrates the degree to which Russia has retained economic links with its former peripheries. While the countries of east-

TABLE 4.2 Power Balance between Russia and Its Neighbors:
Russia's Percentage of Total

	Population			GDP			Armed Forces			Defense Budget		
Year	1995	1997	1999	1995	1997	1999	1995	1997	1999	1995	1997	1999
Russia	50	50	50	90	91	89	65	61	57	95	94	94
Armenia	1	1	1	*	*	*	3	3	4	*	*	*
Azerbaijan	3	3	3	*	*	*	4	3	4	*	*	*
Belarus	3	3	4	2	1	1	4	4	5	*	*	*
Estonia	1	1	*	*	*	*	*	*	*	*	*	*
Georgia	2	2	2	*	*	*	n.a.	2	1	*	*	*
Kazakstan	6	5	5	1	1	2	2	2	4	*	*	*
Kyrgyzstan	2	2	2	*	*	*	*	*	*	*	*	*
Latvia	1	1	1	*	*	*	*	*	*	*	*	*
Lithuania	1	1	1	*	*	*	*	*	*	*	*	*
Moldova	1	1	1	*	*	*	*	*	*	*	*	*
Tajikistan	2	2	2	*	*	*	*	*	*	*	*	*
Turkmenistan	1	2	2	*	*	*	*	*	1	*	*	*
Ukraine	17	17	17	3	4	4	19	19	18	1	2	1
Uzbekistan	8	8	8	1	1	1	1	3	4	*	*	*

Note: Asterisk denotes less than 1 percent. All figures are rounded to the nearest whole number.

Source: International Institute for Strategic Studies, *The Military Balance, 1995–1996* (London: Oxford University Press, 1995), pp. 75–167; *The Military Balance 1997/98* (London: Oxford University Press, 1997), pp. 73–163; *The Military Balance 1999–2000* (London: Oxford University Press, 1999), pp. 79–170.

TABLE 4.3 Russia's Share of Non-Russian States' Trade, 1997

	Imports from Russia as % of Total Imports	Exports to Russia as % of Total Exports	Russia's Percentage of Republics' Trade
Armenia	30	16	19
Azerbaijan	21	21	21
Belarus	63	54	58
Georgia	28	15	18
Kazakstan	34	46	39
Kyrgyzstan	16	29	23
Moldova	62	28	42
Tajikistan	8	15	12
Turkmenistan	n/a	11	n/a
Ukraine	26	47	37
Uzbekistan	n/a	n/a	n/a

Source: Calculated on the basis of figures contained in Lawrence R. Robertson, ed., *Russia and Eurasia Facts and Figures Annual*, vol. 25, pt. 1: *CIS and Russia* (Gulf Breeze, Fla.: Academic International Press, 1999), pp. 40–41.

central Europe and the Baltic have shifted their trade almost entirely away from Russia, many of the non-Russian republics have remained dependent on it. Most dependent are Belarus (with 58 percent of its total trade involving Russia), Moldova (42 percent), Kazakstan (39 percent), and Ukraine (37 percent)—each of which has large Russian-speaking minorities and three of which (Belarus, Kazakstan, and Ukraine) both border on Russia and are among the geographically largest, most populous, and economically most important ex-Soviet republics. Significantly, both Ukraine and Belarus are also highly dependent on energy imports from Russia.[36]

In sum, although few ex-Soviet republics are subordinate to or dependent on Russia across the board, all are, to use Rajan Menon's turn of phrase, "in the shadow of the bear."[37] Only Ukraine remotely compares with Russia in terms of power resources, but its army is in abysmal condition, and its trade and energy dependence nullifies most of its potential for full independence.[38] Turkmenistan, Azerbaijan, Kazakstan, and Uzbekistan are energy independent, and the Baltic states have largely succeeded in decoupling their economies from the former Soviet space, but all are incomparably weaker than Russia.[39] Indeed, the overall level of disparities is so huge that it is inconceivable, at least to me, how they and the resulting dependencies could disappear in the foreseeable future.[40]

Continuity

Revealingly, the boundaries of the USSR's successor states are termed *transparent* by Russians and non-Russians alike. Like most state borders, they are not coterminous with the nations that claim them. Unlike many state boundaries, however, post-Soviet borders—as the products of Soviet administrative, and not planning, priorities—fail even to encompass integrated economic spaces.[41] And inasmuch as most successor states lack a developed state apparatus—that is to say, coherent, complex, and institutionalized Weberian organizations—it is not even clear that their so-called boundaries are the institutionalized features of any kind of entity. Arguably, the boundaries are just cartographic lines, as there is little in the way of distinct entities on either side for them to separate.[42]

As befitted the boundaries of administrative regions, republican borders—as well as the status of some republics—were subject to more than two hundred almost routine alterations from 1921 to 1980.[43] Most changes involved minor border adjustments; some were substantial. For instance, the Karelian Autonomous Soviet Socialist Republic (ASSR) was created in 1923, upgraded to the Karelo-Finnish SSR in 1940, and then demoted to the Karelian ASSR in 1956. The Moldavian ASSR was formed on the left bank of the Dniester River, as part of Ukraine, in 1924, only to be merged with a full-fledged Moldavian SSR located on territories annexed from Romania in 1940. The Ukrainian SSR was expanded to include formerly Polish provinces annexed by Stalin in 1939–1940 and then, in 1954, was bequeathed the Crimea by Nikita Khrushchev. The territory of the later Kazakh SSR went through especially complex permutations involving several name changes as well as transfers and acquisitions of territory.[44]

Not surprisingly, the borders between and among most of the post-Soviet states, and especially between Russia and its neighbors, are minimally guarded and controlled.[45] Although all post-Soviet governments have attempted to introduce customs regimes, they have not been successful in regulating travel and trade and preventing smuggling. Andrea Chandler's description of the situation in Russia applies with equal force to the non-Russian states as well:

> The first problem in customs-control structures is one of chaotic and contradictory state organization. . . . The second, related institutional problem is the weakness of border controls. In countries that are newly setting up customs administration, smuggling problems are to be expected. . . . Under Soviet rule the main purpose of customs officers was to examine passenger luggage and baggage; but in the aftermath of the Soviet collapse the application of customs controls to freight, imports, and exports expanded Russia's customs volume and functions before the country had sufficient capacity to cope with them.[46]

Two factors promote porousness. First, transportation routes—roads, railroads, and air routes—generally connect ex-peripheral states to the former core, Moscow. Thus it is both possible and easy to cross borders. Second, many border regions, especially in Estonia, Latvia, Belarus, Ukraine, and Kazakstan, are populated by Russians or Russian speakers. Indeed, the majority of the twenty-six million ethnic Russians living in the near abroad are concentrated in border areas.[47] Regardless of whether these populations are loyal to their state of residence, are developing separate identities, or pine for annexation, the mere fact that culturally homogeneous populations straddle transparent borders adds to their transparency, makes it more difficult to impose controls, and facilitates the cross-border movement of ideas, goods, practices, norms, and so on.[48] The relationship between the United States and Canada is similar and instructive.

Creeping Reimperialization

It is hard to imagine how the east-central European states could be brought back into a Russian empire. They are independent, they are of strategic importance to the United States and Western Europe, and they are far from the former core. By the same token, Russia's relations with many non-Russian polities in the near abroad so closely approximate the preconditions of reconstitution already described as to lead us to expect some form of reimperialization, probably partial and probably creeping, to take place. Russia already has a central state apparatus; the non-Russians are still in the process of building a central state. Russia has enormous power resources; the non-Russians generally do not. Almost all the non-Russian polities border on Russia. As if that were not enough, many non-Russian states are almost as dependent on Russia economically now as they were in Soviet times. All in all, this set of circumstances would seem to destine the non-Russian states—including, quite possibly, the Balts—for some combination of infor-mally imperial or hegemonic relations.

Were life static, we would have little to add to this picture. But we have no reason not to expect conditions to change internally and externally. Russia and its neighbors may well become relatively weaker or stronger—in terms of state capacity, power resources, and economic strength—in the foresee-able future. Indeed, in the two years after the August 1998 financial crash, Russia experienced substantial economic growth, which, even if unsustain-able in the long run, demonstrates that Russia *can* grow.[49] Because continuity may be held constant, we can imagine nine outcomes of Russia's interaction with its neighbors (see table 4.4).

Not all these outcomes are equally likely. Given the parlous condition of Russia and most of its neighbors after ten years of post-Soviet change, it seems reasonable to conclude that the institutional weight of empire and

TABLE 4.4 Possible Outcomes of Russian–non-Russian Interaction

| | | **Russia** | | |
		Becomes Weaker	Stays the Same	Becomes Stronger
	Become Weaker	*Chaos*	Empire	Empire
Non-Russians	Stay the Same	Independence	*Creeping Re-Imperialization*	Empire
	Become Stronger	Independence	Independence	*Independence*

totalitarianism, and not bad policies and bad leaders making bad choices, best account for their weakness.[50] If so, it is not unreasonable to expect Russia and its neighbors to undergo roughly parallel processes—of weakening, strengthening, or stasis—for the foreseeable future. This suggests that the outcomes on the diagonal formed by italics in table 4.4 are most likely— ceteris paribus, of course. Thus, if all states grow weaker, internal and external chaos is likely to result. If all states grow stronger, then, despite any tensions and conflicts, the non-Russians are likely to retain their independence. If things remain more or less the same as they are, however, creeping reimperialization is likely, because the structural imbalances alone could, by virtue of their force in a geographically contiguous context, push these entities toward one another—quietly, almost stealthily, without military campaigns, expansionist blueprints, and other imperialist paraphernalia.

But other things may not remain equal for three reasons. First, Russia might experience economic recovery sooner and with greater vigor than the other states—partly because of the progress it has already made, partly because of its vast energy resources, and partly because the West has an interest in Russia's recovery.[51] Second, the ineffectiveness and likely demise of the Commonwealth of Independent States (CIS) will facilitate reimperialization.[52] Although non-Russian policy makers generally viewed the CIS as a vehicle for promoting Russian domination—which, to be fair, it probably was—the CIS did, as a multilateral organization, also promote significant relations between and among the non-Russian states—and thus was the very opposite of an empire. If, as seems likely, the CIS fails, political and economic relations between Russia and the non-Russian states will increasingly become bilateral and thus potentially imperial.[53] (President Vladimir Putin's preference for bilateral relations with the non-Russians cannot be considered as corroborating this proposition but as merely reflecting or illustrating underlying structural forces.[54]) With or without the CIS, Belarus may already be on the verge of becoming a Russian province; Armenia, Kazakstan, Tajikistan, and Kyrgyzstan are, for all practical purposes, vassal states.[55]

Third, two strictly exogenous developments—the expansion of the North Atlantic Treaty Organization (NATO) and the European Union (EU) on the one hand and globalization on the other—will in all likelihood accelerate creeping reimperialization. NATO and EU enlargement will, to be sure, remove a variety of east-central European states from Russia's sphere of influence. But enlargement will also create mutually reinforcing institutional boundaries between those countries included in the EU-NATO institutional space — Euroland — and those farther to the east that are excluded therefrom.[56] In turn, we have good reason to believe that most post-Soviet states will be unable to cope with the challenges of globalization. Their isolation from the global economy in general and from Euroland in particular will reinforce East-West cleavages and East-East dependencies. As a result, the most likely outcomes in table 4.4 are located somewhere between the italicized diagonal and the upper-right corner, all involving some form of imperial reconstitution.

EU-NATO Expansion

Baltic, Ukrainian, and other non-Russian policy makers frequently invoke the specter of NATO membership for their states, but one suspects that they must know, as Western policy makers do know, that such an option is not likely for many years to come. First, their militaries, economies, and polities are much too backward; second, many are, as Western policy makers privately concede, not defensible; and third, the West has effectively consigned some to the sphere of influence of what it hopes will be a relatively benign Russia.[57] As a result, although there is hope for Slovakia and Slovenia and a sliver of hope for Romania and Bulgaria, Ukraine, Belarus, Moldova, and the Baltic states are probably fated to remain between two blocs.[58] These blocs may not call themselves blocs, and they may and will sign innumerable documents to settle high-strung non-Russian nerves, but semantic preferences, high-flying phraseology, occasional joint maneuvers, and the very long-term promise of the Partnership for Peace will not change the brute fact that these non-Russians will not be in NATO when it matters most — now and in the near future. Words and activities are no substitute for institutions. In this sense, membership in NATO is a zero-sum game: one is either inside the alliance and embedded in its institutions or outside and left out in the cold.

Although the creation of a security vacuum is an important concern for the states sandwiched between NATO and Russia, the true structural significance of NATO enlargement is, above all, that it deepens the institutional divide between Western Europe and states to the east.[59] Just as the EU is constantly deepening, so too NATO is redefining itself as both a security alliance and a promoter of democracy, human rights, and stability.[60] Increasingly, the EU and NATO may become, as their supporters hope, complementary parts of a "new Europe," with both claiming to be different institutional expressions of the same, as well as same kind of, countries: more or less prosperous and more or less stable industrial democracies that define themselves, and only themselves, as European in culture and spirit.

Protectionist measures related to imports of agricultural products, textiles, metals, and other raw materials already limit east European access to EU markets, but the deepening of the new Europe will create virtually insurmountable barriers to nonmembers.[61] The EU's body of laws, the *acquis communautaire*, consists of about 100,000 pages of rules and regulations affecting all aspects of life of member states—from the shape of bananas to the shape of civil society.[62] Membership in NATO requires a commitment to both democracy and the market, a military capable of being integrated into NATO structures, and an economy strong enough to sustain such a costly effort. With Europe in the process of constructing an interlocking set of highly sophisticated institutions related to democracy, rule of law, civil society, and the market, the expansion of both the EU and NATO into east-central Europe is nothing less than the extension of already formidable European institutional boundaries eastward.[63] And unlike the transparent boundaries between and among the post-Soviet states, those between Euroland and its eastern neighbors will be opaque.[64] Seen in this light, the Schengen Agreement of 1995, which discontinued passport and border controls within Europe while creating legal barriers to the movement of non-EU populations into or through Europe, only formalized the EU's already impassable institutional barriers.[65]

The following example illustrates the logic of the emerging situation. Until 1998 Ukraine and Poland enjoyed unusually close political and economic relations. In particular, Ukrainian laborers and traders could cross into Poland with few restrictions. Not surprisingly, the Polish-Ukrainian border also became a conduit for migrants, refugees, and criminals seeking to enter the European Union.[66] With Poland on the verge of membership in the EU, however, Brussels insisted in 1998 that Poland's border controls be brought in line with Schengen. Warsaw, in turn, informed Kyiv that continued access to Poland for Ukrainians would be contingent on Ukraine's establishing Schengen-like controls on its border with Russia. That Ukraine will fail to establish such controls goes without saying. The boundary is transparent, the cross-border ties are too many and too dense, a Russo-Ukrainian population straddles the border, and the Ukrainian state is too weak to impose such controls or to risk alienating the superpower next door. Once it becomes clear that Ukraine has failed, Poland will have no choice but to comply fully with Schengen and cordon itself off from Ukraine.[67] Bratislava, significantly, abolished visa-free travel to Slovakia for Ukrainians *after* Vladimir Meciar had been deposed, and its chances of EU membership grew accordingly.[68]

Even if Western European policy makers were more than rhetorically committed to expanding the European Union eastward—Germany's former chancellor, Helmut Schmidt, has explicitly stated that Russia, Ukraine, and Belarus do not belong in the EU—only Estonia, Latvia, and Lithuania could possibly be ready for membership in the foreseeable future.[69] All the other post-Soviet states have a rickety government apparatus, minimal rule of law, a depressed and malfunctioning postcommunist economy, a creaky democracy bordering on authoritarianism, and a barely visible civil society. At the same time as most of the postcommunist states are making at best incremental progress toward meeting the membership criteria of EU-NATO, the Euroland states are transforming, or hoping to transform, their own relations both quantitatively and qualitatively. While the East Europeans develop arithmetically, with very low positive slopes at best, the West Europeans are developing exponentially. The developmental gap between Euroland and its eastern neighbors can only grow, while the institutional barriers between them will rise and thicken.

Table 4.5 illustrates the enormity of the EU's institutional distance from the Soviet successor states. I have modified the ratings developed by Freedom House to measure institutional development in eight categories—political process, civil society, independent media, governance and public administration, rule of law, privatization, macroeconomics, and microeconomics. On my modified scale, 1 represents the least development and 7 the most development. I have then added the ratings to convey the degree of interconnectedness between and among institutions and to stress that, taken together, they constitute a coherent whole.

To denote ongoing institutional change, I assigned the countries that belong to the EU scores of 56 (7×8) for 1997, 60 (7.5×8) for 1998, and 64 (8×8) for 2000. Once the euro becomes a common currency in 2002, the European economies become even more integrated, and further steps are taken to promote common judicial, legal, and political norms and policies—even if they stop far short of European statehood or federation—the EU's score is likely to jump to 72 (9×8) and in time to 80 (10×8). In contrast, unless we believe that the post-Soviet states are likely to experience sudden economic and political takeoffs anytime soon—and the stability of their scores militates against such a conclusion—all but the Balts are likely to remain in the 10–35 range for years to come.

TABLE 4.5 Institutional Distance Between Euroland and the Post-Soviet States

Year	2000	1998	1997
Euroland	64	60	56
Estonia	48	48	47
Latvia	46	46	46
Lithuania	46	47	46
Georgia	33	29	28
Moldova	33	32	33
Armenia	30	28	29
Russia	30	32	34
Ukraine	29	29	31
Kyrgyzstan	28	29	30
Kazakstan	24	24	24
Azerbaijan	22	21	21
Tajikistan	18	16	15
Belarus	13	14	17
Uzbekistan	13	13	14
Turkmenistan	10	10	11

Note: All figures have been rounded to the nearest whole number. Because the 1997 ratings had only one number for the economy, I multiplied it by 2 to make the figures consistent with those for 1998 and 2000.

Source: Adrian Karatnycky, Alexander J. Motyl, and Boris Shor, eds., *Nations in Transit, 1997* (New Brunswick, N.J.: Transaction, 1997); Adrian Karatnycky, Alexander J. Motyl, and Charles Graybow, eds., *Nations in Transit, 1998* (New Brunswick, N.J.: Transaction, 1999); Adrian Karatnycky, Alexander J. Motyl, and Aili Piano, eds., *Nations in Transit, 1999–2000* (New Brunswick, N.J.: Transaction, 2000).

Globalization

Globalization will prove to be equally devastating for most of the Soviet successor states. Although scholars disagree on what exactly globalization is and when it began, they do seem to agree that globalization involves flows of information, goods, people, and resources across state boundaries and that

these flows, which probably began no later than the nineteenth century as
by-products of capitalism and imperialism, have recently accelerated.[70] Put
this way, today's version of globalization amounts to a spin-off of untram-
meled capitalism and rampant modernization. Edward Luttwak's term,
turbo-capitalism, may therefore be a more accurate designation for ongoing
processes in the world economy.[71] It may also be more helpful in enabling
us to appreciate why the Soviet successor states are unlikely to fare well.
Backwardness may have advantages, as Alexander Gerschenkron once maintained, but it is hard to see just what the advantages of failed socialism could
be in an unremittingly and mercilessly capitalist world.[72]

Tables 4.6, 4.7, 4.8, and 4.9, which measure the competitiveness of the
post-Soviet economies, the level of their perceived corruption, their openness, and their economic creativity, provide a good sense of how far they are
from meeting the challenges of the global economy.

Significantly, Russia and Ukraine score abysmally low on all four indexes;
the five Central Asian and three Caucasus states score equally low, or lower,
if and when they appear in a rating; Bulgaria is also no stand-out; if better
data existed, Belarus and Yugoslavia would surely figure as among the very
least competitive, open, and creative and among the very most corrupt. If
these four indexes are broadly reflective of a country's ability to cope with
globalization, the post-Soviet states will, to put things bluntly, be globalization's losers—at least in the foreseeable future. As such, they will suffer
several consequences. First, they will recede institutionally even further from
the states grouped within the European Union. As Euroland's institutions
respond and adapt to globalization more or less successfully, those of the
East will either stagnate, relatively, or experience indigenous forms of development different from and perhaps even inimical to those in the EU.[73]
Second, their incapacity to compete in the global economy will reduce their
chances of embarking on and adopting successful market-oriented economic
reform. As a result, a tendency to seek "third ways" involving greater state
intervention is likely to take hold. Authoritarian solutions are especially likely
if and when relative economic stagnation continues and "confining conditions" appear to require "revolutionary breakthroughs."[74] Third, both developments are likely to increase the isolation of these countries from more
developed countries and their dependence on one another—and especially
on Russia, the former core and current military and economic power.[75]

That dependence, as we know from tables 4.2 and 4.3, is already quite
high. Some post-Soviet states, such as Estonia, Latvia, and Lithuania, are

TABLE 4.6 Competitiveness Ratings, 1999

Singapore (highest score)	2.12
United States	1.58
Average of top 15 countries	1.25
European Union	0.57
East-Central Europe	-0.74
Hungary	-0.39
Czech Republic	-0.4
Poland	-0.67
Slovakia	-0.72
Bulgaria	-1.5
Ukraine	-1.94
Russia (lowest score)	-2.02

Note: The top fifteen countries are Singapore, the United States, Hong Kong, Taiwan, Canada, Switzerland, Luxembourg, the United Kingdom, the Netherlands, Ireland, Finland, Australia, New Zealand, Japan, and Norway. The east-central European or post-Soviet countries given here are the only ones listed in the report.

Source: World Economic Forum, Global Competitiveness Report, 1999 <<http://www.weforum.org/publications/GCR/99rankings.asp>> (November 15, 1999).

likely to cope with globalization satisfactorily and thus to leave the sphere of Russia's economic influence. Belarus, Ukraine, Moldova, Armenia, Georgia, Azerbaijan, and the five Central Asian states are as unlikely as Russia to transform their polities, economies, societies, and cultures in the thorough manner that global competitiveness supposedly requires. Worse, if they attempt to do so rapidly and comprehensively, they will in fact be embarking on revolution from above or courting revolution from below. And no inductive or deductive grounds exist for expecting anything but calamity to result from such adventures.[76] In any case, societal breakdown and state failure will not enhance these countries' ability to compete in global markets.

TABLE 4.7 Corruption Perceptions Index, 1998–1999

	1999	1998
Average of top 15 countries	8.9	9.0
European Union	7.6	7.6
United States	7.5	7.5
East-Central Europe/Balts	3.8	
Ex-Soviet States	2.4	
Slovenia	6.0	
Estonia	5.7	5.7
Hungary	5.2	5.0
Czech Republic	4.6	4.8
Poland	4.2	4.6
Lithuania	3.8	
Slovakia	3.7	3.9
Belarus	3.4	3.9
Latvia	3.4	2.7
Bulgaria	3.3	2.9
Macedonia	3.3	
Romania	3.3	3.0
Croatia	2.7	
Moldova	2.6	
Ukraine	2.6	2.8
Armenia	2.5	
Russia	2.4	2.4
Albania	2.3	
Georgia	2.3	
Kazakstan	2.3	
Kyrgyzstan	2.2	
Yugoslavia	2.0	3.0
Uzbekistan	1.8	
Azerbaijan	1.7	

Note: A score of 10 "represents a perceived level of negligible bribery," whereas zero "represents responses indicating very high levels of bribery." The 1998 index did not survey all the countries included in the 1999 index. The top fifteen countries are Sweden, Australia, Canada, Austria, Switzerland, the Netherlands, the United Kingdom, Belgium, Germany, the United States, Singapore, Spain, France, Japan, and Malaysia.

Source: Transparency International, *The Transparency International 1999 Corruption Perceptions Index*; *The Transparency International 1998 Corruption Perceptions Index* <<wysiwyg:// 4//http://www.transparency.de/documents/cpi/index.html>> (November 18, 1999).

TABLE 4.8 Openness of Emerging Markets, 2000

Singapore (highest score/most open)	86
Estonia	78
Average of top ten countries	77
Slovenia	74
Lithuania	73
Latvia	70
Romania	70
Hungary	66
Czech Republic	60
Poland	60
Bulgaria	57
Slovakia	52
Russia	52
Ukraine	48
Uzbekistan	32

Note: Because the "scores represent the averaged sum of the 0–10 scores a country received on each of the 16 areas of market openness," the highest score possible is 160. The top ten countries are Singapore, Chile, Hong Kong, Estonia, Peru, Slovenia, South Africa, Lithuania, Venezuela, and Taiwan.

Source: Tuck School of Business, Emerging Markets Access Index, 2000, <<http://www.dartmouth.edu/tuck/news/media/pr20000525_emai.html>> (June 14, 2000).

In sum, the deepening and broadening of EU-NATO will, in conjunction with globalization, divide Europe into vastly different, perhaps even incompatible, halves. And in the Europe to the east of Euroland, states will, ceteris paribus, have no alternative to accepting the reality of relative Russian dominance and their own economic dependence on one another and, above all, on Russia. A hublike structure could take shape if individual non-Russian states are compelled to confront their isolation from the world and their

TABLE 4.9 Economic Creativity Index, 2000

United States (highest score)	2.02
Average of the top 15 countries	1.38
European Union	0.85
Hungary	0.66
Poland	0.56
Czech Republic	-0.15
Slovakia	-0.29
Russia	-0.90
Ukraine	-1.21
Bulgaria	-1.43

Note: The top fifteen countries are the United States, Finland, Singapore, Luxembourg, Sweden, Israel, Ireland, the Netherlands, the United Kingdom, Iceland, Switzerland, Hong Kong, Denmark, Germany, and Canada.

Source: World Economic Forum, *Global Competitiveness Report* <<http://www.weforum.org/ reports_pub.nsf/Documents//Home + − + Reports + and + Publication + − + Competitiveness + − + Competitiveness + Report + − + Economic + Creativity + Index>> (September 25, 2000).

dependence on Russia by either institutionalizing that dependence and/or by transforming their relations with Russia into the centerpiece of their foreign policy.[77] Johan Galtung almost certainly overstates the case by arguing that "today Russia is an ordinary, expansionist occidental country, and a minimum concrete agenda would be based on Slavic culture and religious orthodoxy, building a Soviet Union II based on Russia, Belarus, eastern Ukraine and northern Kazakhstan."[78] Rather more likely is that reimperialization—quiet and evolutionary—is likely in some parts of the former USSR and that hegemony is a sure bet for most of Russia's neighbors.[79]

Conclusion: Losing Empire

Although some non-Russian states may have no choice but to engage in what Karen Dawisha calls "autocolonization," such an outcome will be stable beyond the short run only if the Russian state is strong enough to sustain it.[1] And that of course is a big if. Empire presupposes that the core elite is able to marshal resources and information from the periphery and to funnel them toward a variety of imperial ends. At present and for the foreseeable future, however, the Russian state is too fragmented and too weak to enable the Russian elite to play such an extractive and coordinating role effectively vis-à-vis the Russian Federation's own ethnofederal units and even more so with respect to other entities.[2] Not only is a renewed Russian empire almost certain not to be a replica of the Soviet Union but it is likely to emerge in a condition of advanced decay and thus be especially prone to attrition.

How could such a decaying and declining imperial system not succumb to attrition? Of the four intervening factors discussed in chapter 3, two do not apply and two might. Totalitarian political controls are too expensive to be revived, whereas geopolitical isolation and external noninterference would be irrelevant to an empire suffering from such advanced decay. Strategic alliances with great powers, such as the United States or NATO, are possible, if far-fetched, but unlikely to stem disintegration in so vast a geographic space as Russia. Only Russia's enormous natural resources could — especially with the assistance of solicitous Western firms — generate sufficient easy money to keep energy-dependent polities in the fold, maintain a large or effective military, and hold the empire together.[3]

More important, so brittle an imperial entity will be especially susceptible to all manner of shocks, even relatively minor ones. Although it is impossible to predict when such stress surges will strike, we can imagine that they will involve drastic reductions in easy money, perhaps as a result of falling energy prices, and/or in the continued, or growing, refusal of the Russian Federation's regions and republics to pay taxes to a core that may not be able to compel them to do so anyway. Either way, such an empire would not survive. Indeed, it is not inconceivable that an imperial state so brittle yet so over-extended could even disintegrate.[4] Only if partial reimperialization were to creep into place during the next two to three decades, thereby enabling Russia to grow stronger relative to the non-Russians, could it avoid advanced decay, brittleness, and well-nigh inevitable collapse.

Although the Russian state's collapse may be good news for non-Russian nationalists, the disintegration of a decaying empire and huge state is unlikely to be entirely peaceful. One need not be a pessimist to suspect that the stability and security of Russia, its neighbors, and Western Europe can only deteriorate.[5] Is there no alternative to this gloomy forecast? Several, even gloomier, possibilities exist. If the Czech Republic, Hungary, and especially Poland fail to join the European Union before, say, 2005, the total overlap of political and economic institutions I referred to earlier may be delayed for some years.[6] If the European Monetary Union produces social distress, economic dislocations, and political infighting, Euroland could turn into an awkward amalgam of squabbling states.[7] And if, in addition to Bosnia and Kosovo, NATO experiences a few more blows to its self-esteem, it too might lose its élan.[8] If any or all of these eventualities come to pass—and the odds may not be quite as long as they seem—Euroland's expansion would be far less significant institutionally than I have suggested. Alternatively, if Russia becomes outwardly imperialist, NATO is likely to respond by bringing the Baltic states and even Ukraine into its fold.

Because structural conditions are not amenable to easy change, and because the deepening and widening of NATO and the EU appear to have acquired their own irresistible momentum, the stability and security of East and West may have become mutually exclusive. Imperial collapse, Russia's disintegration, and the unremittingly unhappy consequences thereof may therefore be forestalled if European integration stalls or if Russia turns nasty. Although such a trade-off is to no one's ultimate benefit, it appears to be the only way out of the cul de sac created by postimperial conditions in the East and post–cold war developments in the West. The only alternative to the fire may, alas, be the relative comfort of the frying pan. Ceteris paribus, of course.

Notes

All translations from foreign-language sources are mine.

Introduction: Finding Empire

1. See Michael Hardt and Antonio Negri, *Empire* (Cambridge, Mass.: Harvard University Press, 2000), for a philosophically grounded discussion of empire in the age of globalization.
2. S. N. Eisenstadt, introduction to S. N. Eisenstadt, ed., *The Decline of Empires* (Englewood Cliffs, N. J.: Prentice-Hall, 1967), p. 4.
3. A few examples will convey the richness of the extant historical literature: Warren Treadgold, *A History of the Byzantine State and Society* (Palo Alto, Calif.: Stanford University Press, 1997); John Strachey, *The End of Empire* (New York: Praeger, 1959); René Grousset, *The Empire of the Steppes* (New Brunswick, N.J.: Rutgers University Press, 1970); Eric Hobsbawm, *The Age of Empire, 1875–1914* (New York: Pantheon, 1987); Robert Kann, *A History of the Habsburg Empire, 1526–1918* (Berkeley: University of California Press, 1974); Franz Ansprenger, *The Dissolution of the Colonial Empires* (London: Routledge, 1989); A. B. Bosworth, *Conquest and Empire: The Reign of Alexander the Great* (Cambridge: Cambridge University Press, 1988); D. W. Meinig, *The Shaping of America: Continental America, 1800–1867*, vol. 2 (New Haven, Conn.: Yale University Press, 1993); David Good, *The Economic Rise of the Habsburg Empire, 1750–1914* (Berkeley: University of California Press, 1984); D. K. Fieldhouse, *Economics and Empire, 1830–1914* (Ithaca, N.Y.: Cornell University

Press, 1973). And of course Edward Gibbon, *Decline and Fall of the Roman Empire* (New York: Viking, 1952).

4. See Geoffrey W. Conrad and Arthur A. Demarest, *Religion and Empire: The Dynamics of Aztec and Inca Expansionism* (Cambridge: Cambridge University Press, 1984); Joseph Tainter, *The Collapse of Complex Societies* (Cambridge: Cambridge University Press, 1988); Norman Yoffee and George L. Cowgill, eds., *The Collapse of Ancient States and Civilizations* (Tucson: University of Arizona Press, 1988); Norman Hammond, *Ancient Maya Civilization* (New Brunswick, N.J.: Rutgers University Press, 1988).

5. Robert Gilpin, *War and Change in World Politics* (Cambridge: Cambridge University Press, 1981); George Lichtheim, *Imperialism* (New York: Praeger, 1971); David A. Lake, "Anarchy, Hierarchy, and the Variety of International Relations," *International Organization* 50 (winter 1996): 1–33; Wolfgang J. Mommsen, *Theories of Imperialism* (New York: Random House, 1980); Charles A. Kupchan, *The Vulnerability of Empire* (Ithaca, N.Y.: Cornell University Press, 1994); Jack Snyder, *Myths of Empire* (Ithaca, N.Y.: Cornell University Press, 1991); Alexander Cooley, "Explaining Imperial Persistence and Decline: Contemporary Dependencies, Asset Specificity, and Global Economic Change," paper presented at the annual convention of the American Political Science Association, September 3–6, 1998, Boston; Mark N. Katz, "The Legacy of Empire in International Relations," *Comparative Strategy* 12 (1993): 365–83.

6. Michael W. Doyle, *Empires* (Ithaca, N.Y.: Cornell University Press, 1986); S. N. Eisenstadt, "Center-Periphery Relations in the Soviet Empire," in Alexander J. Motyl, ed., *Thinking Theoretically About Soviet Nationalities: History and Comparison in the Study of the USSR*, pp. 205–21 (New York: Columbia University Press, 1992); Karen Dawisha and Bruce Parrott, eds., *The End of Empire? The Transformation of the USSR in Comparative Perspective* (Armonk, N.Y.: Sharpe, 1997); Alexander Demandt, ed., *Das Ende der Weltreiche: Von den Persen bis zur Sowjetunion* (Munich: Beck, 1997); Richard Lorenz, ed., *Das Verdämmern der Macht: Vom Untergang grosser Reiche* (Frankfurt am Main: Fischer Taschenbuch Verlag, 2000); Robert A. Kann, *The Habsburg Empire: A Study in Integration and Disintegration* (New York: Praeger, 1957); Carlo M. Cipolla, ed., *The Economic Decline of Empires* (London: Methuen, 1970); Christopher Chase-Dunn and Thomas D. Hall, *Rise and Demise: Comparing World Systems* (Boulder, Colo.: Westview, 1997); Robert Wesson, *The Imperial Order* (Berkeley: University of California Press, 1967); Karen Barkey and Mark von Hagen, eds., *After Empire: Multiethnic Societies and Nation Building* (Boulder, Colo.: Westview, 1997); Rupert Emerson, *From Empire to Nation* (Boston: Beacon, 1960); S. N. Eisenstadt, *The Political Systems of Empires* (Glencoe, N.Y.: Free Press, 1963); John H. Kautsky, *The Politics of Aristocratic*

Empires (Chapel Hill: University of North Carolina Press, 1982); S. E. Finer, *The History of Government*, vols. 1–3 (Oxford: Oxford University Press, 1997).

7. See Paul Kennedy, *The Rise and Decline of the Great Powers* (New York: Vintage, 1987); Geir Lundestad, *The American "Empire"* (Oslo: Norwegian University Press, 1990); Imanuel Geiss, "Great Powers and Empires: Historical Mechanisms of Their Making and Breaking," in Geir Lundestad, ed., *The Fall of Great Powers: Peace, Stability, and Legitimacy*, pp. 23–46 (Oslo: Scandinavian University Press, 1994).

8. See Richard Koebner, *Empire* (New York: Grosset and Dunlop, 1965), pp. 1–60.

9. For exceptions to this rule, see Alexander Wendt and Daniel Friedheim, "Hierarchy Under Anarchy: Informal Empire and the East German State," *International Organization* 49 (autumn 1995): 689–721; Rey Koslowski and Friedrich V. Kratochwil, "Understanding Change in International Politics: The Soviet Empire's Demise and the International System," *International Organization* 48 (spring 1994): 215–47; Rodney Bruce Hall, *National Collective Identity: Social Constructs and International Systems* (New York: Columbia University Press, 1999).

10. Yale H. Ferguson and Richard W. Mansbach, *Polities: Authority, Identities, and Change* (Columbia: University of South Carolina Press, 1996).

11. Leonard Binder et al., eds., *Crises and Sequences of Political Development* (Princeton, N.J.: Princeton University Press, 1971). See also Daniel Lerner, *The Passing of Traditional Society* (Glencoe, Ill.: Free Press, 1958); Karl Deutsch, "Social Mobilization and Political Development," *American Political Science Review* 55 (September 1961): 493–514; Edward A. Shils, *Political Development in the New States* (The Hague: Mouton, 1962). For a critique, see Irene L. Gendzier, *Managing Political Change: Social Scientists and the Third World* (Boulder, Colo.: Westview, 1985).

12. The transitions literature is enormous and growing. See in particular Juan Linz and Alfred Stepan, *Problems of Democratic Transition and Consolidation: Southern Europe, South America, and Post-Communist Europe* (Baltimore, Md.: Johns Hopkins University Press, 1996); Mary Ellen Fischer, ed., *Establishing Democracies* (Boulder, Colo.: Westview, 1996); Lisa Anderson, ed., *Transitions to Democracy* (New York: Columbia University Press, 1999). For a good review of the literature, see Georg Sørensen, *Democracy and Democratization: Processes and Prospects in a Changing World* (Boulder, Colo.: Westview, 1993).

13. See Robert Conquest, ed., *The Last Empire: Nationality and the Soviet Future* (Palo Alto, Calif.: Hoover Institution Press, 1986); Henry S. Rowen and Charles Wolf Jr., eds., *The Future of the Soviet Empire* (New York: St. Martin's, 1987); David J. Dallin, *The New Soviet Empire* (New Haven, Conn.: Yale University Press, 1951).

14. Ariel Cohen, *Russian Imperialism: Development and Crisis* (Westport, Conn.:
     Praeger, 1996), pp. 151–52; Alexander J. Motyl, "The End of Sovietology: From
     Soviet Studies to Post-Soviet Studies," in Alexander J. Motyl, ed., *The Post-
     Soviet Nations: Perspectives on the Demise of the USSR*, pp. 302–14 (New York:
     Columbia University Press, 1992); Giovanni Sartori, "Totalitarianism, Model
     Mania, and Learning from Error," *Journal of Theoretical Politics* 5 (1993): 5–
     22; Abbott Gleason, *Totalitarianism: The Inner History of the Cold War* (New
     York: Oxford University Press, 1995).
15. See V. I. Lenin, "Imperialism: The Highest Stage of Capitalism," *Selected
     Works in One Volume*, pp. 169–263 (New York: International Publishers, 1971);
     J. A. Hobson, *Imperialism: A Study* (London: Allen and Unwin, 1905); Rudolf
     Hilferding, *Das Finanzkapital* (Vienna: Wienervolksbuchhandlung, 1910).
     See also Winfried Baumgart, *Imperialism: The Idea and Reality of British and
     French Colonial Expansion, 1880–1914* (Oxford: Oxford University Press,
     1982); V. G. Kiernan, *Imperialism and Its Contradictions* (New York: Rout-
     ledge, 1995); Fieldhouse, *Economics and Empire*, pp. 38–62.
16. Jeremy Azrael, ed., *Soviet Nationality Policies and Practices* (New York: Prae-
     ger, 1978); Seweryn Bialer, "How Russians Rule Russia," *Problems of Com-
     munism* 15 (September–October 1964): 45–52; "Nationalities and Nation-
     alism in the USSR: Special Issue," *Problems of Communism* 16 (September–
     October 1967); Bohdan Nahaylo and Victor Swoboda, *Soviet Disunion: A
     History of the Nationalities Problem in the USSR* (New York: Free Press,
     1990); Gerhard Simon, *Nationalism and Policy Toward the Nationalities in
     the Soviet Union* (Boulder, Colo.: Westview, 1991); Alexandre Bennigsen and
     S. Enders Wimbush, *Muslim National Communism in the Soviet Union* (Chi-
     cago: University of Chicago Press, 1979); Alexander J. Motyl, *Will the Non-
     Russians Rebel? State, Ethnicity, and Stability in the USSR* (Ithaca, N.Y.:
     Cornell University Press, 1980); Alexander J. Motyl, "'Sovietology in One
     Country' or Comparative Nationality Studies?" *Slavic Review* 48 (spring
     1989): 83–88; Motyl, *Thinking Theoretically About Soviet Nationalities*; Ed-
     ward Allworth, ed., *Soviet Nationality Problems* (New York: Columbia Uni-
     versity Press, 1971); Alexandre Bennigsen and Marie Broxup, *The Islamic
     Threat to the Soviet State* (London: Croom Helm, 1983); Michael Rywkin,
     Moscow's Muslim Challenge (Armonk, N.Y.: Sharpe, 1982); S. Enders Wim-
     bush, ed., *Soviet Nationalities in Strategic Perspective* (London: Croom Helm,
     1985).
17. Hélène Carrère d'Encausse, *Decline of an Empire: The Soviet Socialist Repub-
     lics in Revolt* (New York: Newsweek Books, 1979). See also Marco Buttino, ed.,
     *In a Collapsing Empire: Underdevelopment, Ethnic Conflicts, and Nationalism
     in the Soviet Union* (Milan: Feltrinelli, 1993); Alvin Gouldner, "Stalinism: A
     Study in Internal Colonialism," *Telos* 10 (winter 1977–78): 5–48.

18. See Charles F. Furtado Jr. and Andrea Chandler, eds., *Perestroika in the Soviet Republics: Documents on the National Question* (Boulder, Colo.: Westview, 1992). Some Soviet analysts were also involved in relegitimizing the concept of totalitarianism. See Georgii Arbatov and E. Batalov, "Politicheskaia reforma: evoliutsiia sovetskogo gosudarstva," *Kommunist* (March 1989): 35–46; Valerii Tishkov, "Narody i gosudarstvo," *Kommunist* (January 1989): 49–59; A. A. Kara-Murza and A. K. Voskresenskii, eds., *Totalitarizm kak istoricheskii fenomen* (Moscow: Filosofskoe obshchestvo SSSR, 1989).

19. Valerie Bunce used imperial terminology several years before the USSR's collapse. See Bunce, "The Empire Strikes Back: The Evolution of the Eastern Bloc from a Soviet Asset to a Soviet Liability," *International Organization* 39 (winter 1985): 1–46.

20. Mark Beissinger, "The Persisting Ambiguity of Empire," *Post-Soviet Affairs* 11 (1995): 149–57.

21. See Alexander J. Motyl, *Revolutions, Nations, Empires: Conceptual Limits and Theoretical Possibilities* (New York: Columbia University Press, 1999), pp. 1–15.

22. Giovanni Sartori, "Guidelines for Concept Analysis," in Giovanni Sartori, ed., *Social Science Concepts*, pp. 15–85 (Beverly Hills, Calif.: Sage, 1984); Motyl, *Revolutions, Nations, Empires*, pp. 8–15.

23. Oswald Spengler, *The Decline of the West* (New York: Modern Library, 1932). See also Arnold Toynbee, *A Study of History* (New York: Weathervane, 1972); H. Stuart Hughes, *Consciousness and Society: The Reorientation of European Social Thought, 1890–1930* (New York: Vintage, 1958); Pieter Geyl, *Debates with Historians* (New York: Meridian, 1971), pp. 150–64.

24. Francis Fukuyama, "The End of History?" in Fareed Zakaria, ed., *The New Shape of World Politics*, pp. 1–27 (New York: Foreign Affairs, 1997).

25. Hughes, *Consciousness and Society*; Robert M. Adams, *Decadent Societies* (San Francisco, Calif.: North Point, 1983); Brooks Adams, *The Law of Civilization and Decay* (New York: Knopf, 1943).

26. See Theo Sommer, "Europa im Aufbruch," *Die Zeit*, January 5, 2000, p. 4; Bill Emmott, "The Twentieth Century," *Economist*, September 11, 1999, pp. 5–44. See especially Zygmunt Bauman, *Modernity and the Holocaust* (Ithaca, N.Y.: Cornell University Press, 1989), and Dan Smith, ed., *The State of War and Peace Atlas*, rev. 3d ed. (London: Penguin, 1997).

27. See John Barrow, *Theories of Everything: The Quest for Ultimate Explanation* (New York: Fawcett Columbine, 1991); Motyl, *Revolutions, Nations, Empires*, pp. 9–11.

28. See Yale Ferguson and Richard Mansbach, *The State, Conceptual Chaos, and the Future of International Relations Theory* (Boulder, Colo.: Rienner, 1989); Motyl, *Revolutions, Nations, Empires*, pp. 132–33.

29. Johan Galtung, "A Structural Theory of Imperialism," *Journal of Peace Research* 8 (1971): 81–117.

30. Karl Deutsch, "Cracks in the Monolith: Possibilities and Patterns of Disintegration in Totalitarian Systems," in Harry Eckstein and David E. Apter, eds., *Comparative Politics: A Reader*, pp. 497–508 (New York: Free Press, 1963).

31. Rein Taagepera, "Expansion and Contraction Patterns of Large Polities: Context for Russia," *International Studies Quarterly* 41 (1997): 475–504; Taagepera, "Size and Duration of Empires: Growth-Decline Curves, 600 B.C. to 600 A.D.," *Social Science History* 3 (October 1979): 115–38; Taagepera, "Size and Duration of Empires: Systematics of Size," *Social Science Research* 7 (1978): 108–27; Taagepera, "Size and Duration of Empires: Growth-Decline Curves, 3000 to 600 B.C.," *Social Science Research* 7 (1978): 180–96.

32. That imperial trajectories also resemble the trajectories of great powers is not surprising: after all, empires *are* great powers. This resemblance permits us to treat the former as a species of the latter. But it does not compel us to do so any more than the similarity between empires and federations or between political empires and business empires forces us to pay it exclusive theoretical attention. We can just as easily, and legitimately, treat empires as entities unto themselves and attempt to understand them on their own terms.

33. On algorithmic compressibility see Barrow, *Theories of Everything*, pp. 14–20.

34. James Fearon, "Counterfactuals and Hypothesis Testing in Political Science," *World Politics* 43 (January 1991): 169–95.

35. Nelson Goodman, *Fact, Fiction, and Forecast* (Cambridge, Mass.: Harvard University Press, 1983). See also Philip E. Tetlock and Aaron Belkin, eds., *Counterfactual Thought Experiments in World Politics* (Princeton, N.J.: Princeton University Press, 1996).

36. See Carl Hempel, *Aspects of Scientific Explanation and Other Essays in the Philosophy of Science* (New York: Free Press, 1965); Ernst Nagel, *The Structure of Science*, 2d ed. (Indianapolis, Ind.: Hackett, 1977).

37. On intervening variables see Robert Audi, ed., *The Cambridge Dictionary of Philosophy* (Cambridge: Cambridge University Press, 1995), p. 382.

38. Alexander J. Motyl, "Why Empires Reemerge: Imperial Collapse and Imperial Revival in Comparative Perspective," *Comparative Politics* 31 (January 1999): 127–45.

39. Alexander J. Motyl, "After Empire: Competing Discourses and Interstate Conflict in Postimperial Eastern Europe," in Barnett Rubin and Jack Snyder, eds., *Post-Soviet Political Order: Conflict and State Building*, pp. 14–33 (London: Routledge, 1998); Motyl, "Imperial Collapse and Revolutionary Change: Austria-Hungary, Tsarist Russia, and the Soviet Empire," in Jürgen Nautz and Richard Vahrenkamp, eds., *Die Wiener Jahrhundertwende*, pp. 813–32 (Vienna: Böhlau, 1993); Motyl, "From Imperial Decay to Imperial Collapse: The Fall

of the Soviet Empire in Comparative Perspective," in Richard Rudolph and David Good, eds., *Nationalism and Empire: The Habsburg Monarchy and the Soviet Union*, pp. 15–43 (New York: St. Martin's, 1991).

40. Motyl, *Revolutions, Nations, Empires*, pp. 11–18.
41. See Giovanni Sartori, "Concept Misformation in Comparative Politics," *American Political Science Review* 64 (December 1970): 1033–53; Sartori, "Comparing and Miscomparing," *Journal of Theoretical Politics* 3 (1991): 243–57.
42. See "The Role of Theory in Comparative Politics: A Symposium," *World Politics* 48 (October 1995): 1–49; Thomas A. Spragens Jr., *The Dilemma of Contemporary Political Theory* (New York: Dunellen, 1973); Douglas Chalmers, "Interpretive Frameworks: A Structure of Theory in Political Science," unpublished paper, 1987.
43. See, for instance, Ian S. Lustick's devastating critique of the work of Arend Lijphart: "Lijphart, Lakatos, and Consociationalism," *World Politics* 50 (October 1997): 88–117.

1. Imperial Beginnings

1. Johan Galtung, "A Structural Theory of Imperialism," *Journal of Peace Research* 8 (1971): 8.
2. Ibid., pp. 82–83.
3. Ibid., p. 85.
4. Alexander J. Motyl, "Thinking About Empire," in Karen Barkey and Mark von Hagen, eds., *After Empire: Multiethnic Societies and Nation Building*, pp. 19–29 (Boulder, Colo.: Westview, 1997). Michael Doyle disagrees with this argument. See *Empires* (Ithaca, N.Y.: Cornell University Press, 1986), p. 34.
5. Galtung, "Structural Theory of Imperialism," pp. 83, 89.
6. The presence of culturally distinct populations, the non-natives and natives, does not preclude ethnic, cultural, or religious diversity. For a discussion of ethnic diversity of the Ottoman core, see Justin McCarthy, *Muslims and Minorities: The Population of Ottoman Anatolia and the End of the Empire* (New York: New York University Press, 1983). On culturally distinct populations see Donald J. Puchala, "International Encounters of Another Kind," *Global Society* 11 (1997): 5–29; Rushton Coulborn, "Structure and Process in the Rise and Fall of Civilized Societies," *Comparative Studies in Society and History* 8 (1965–1966): 404–31.
7. Alexander J. Motyl, *Revolutions, Nations, Empires: Conceptual Limits and Theoretical Possibilities* (New York: Columbia University Press, 1999), pp. 118–

22. See also Jean Gottmann, ed., *Centre and Periphery: Spatial Variation in Politics* (Beverly Hills, Calif.: Sage, 1980).

8. D. W. Meinig, *The Shaping of America: Atlantic America, 1492–1800*, vol. 1 (New Haven, Conn.: Yale University Press, 1986), p. 370. See also Geoffrey Parker, *The Geopolitics of Domination* (London: Routledge, 1988), pp. 66–75.

9. Gary B. Miles, "Roman and Modern Imperialism: A Reassessment," *Comparative Studies in Society and History* 32 (October 1990): 641.

10. C. Wright Mills, *The Power Elite* (New York: Oxford University Press, 1959); John A. Armstrong, "Administrative Elites in Multiethnic Polities," *International Political Science Review* 1 (1980): 107–28. See also John A. Armstrong, *The European Administrative Elite* (Princeton, N.J.: Princeton University Press, 1973).

11. Carter V. Findley, *Bureaucratic Reform in the Ottoman Empire: The Sublime Porte, 1789–1922* (Princeton, N.J.: Princeton University Press, 1980), pp. 12, 15. See also Michael Ursinus, "Byzanz, Osmanisches Reich, türkischer Nationalstaat: Zur Gleichzeitichkeit des Ungleichzeitigen am Vorabend des Ersten Weltkriegs," in Richard Lorenz, ed., *Das Verdämmern der Macht: Vom Untergang grosser Reiche* (Frankfurt am Main: Fischer Taschenbuch Verlag, 2000), p. 153.

12. See Cho-yun Hsu, "The Roles of the Literati and of Regionalism in the Fall of the Han Dynasty," in Norman Yoffee and George L. Cowgill, eds., *The Collapse of Ancient States and Civilizations*, pp. 176–95 (Tucson: University of Arizona Press, 1988).

13. See Michael Voslensky, *Nomenklatura: The Soviet Ruling Class* (New York: Doubleday, 1984); Seweryn Bialer, *Stalin's Successors: Leadership, Stability, and Change in the Soviet Union* (Cambridge: Cambridge University Press, 1980); Jerry Hough, *The Soviet Prefects* (Cambridge, Mass.: Harvard University Press, 1969).

14. Bruce Parrott, "Analyzing the Transformation of the Soviet Union in Comparative Perspective," in Karen Dawisha and Bruce Parrott, eds., *The End of Empire? The Transformation of the USSR in Comparative Perspective* (Armonk, N.Y.: Sharpe, 1997), p. 7.

15. Galtung, "Structural Theory of Imperialism," p. 89.

16. Gerhard Masur, *Simon Bolivar* (Albuquerque: University of New Mexico Press, 1948), p. 678, is quoted in Benedict Anderson, *Imagined Communities* (London: Verso, 1983), p. 54. See also Hans-Joachim König, "Der Zerfall des Spanischen Weltreichs in Amerika: Ursachen und Folgen," in Lorenz, *Das Verdämmern der Macht*, p. 133.

17. Meinig, *Shaping of America*, vol. 1, p. 378.

18. On vagueness as a philosophical problem see Linda C. Burns, *Vagueness: An Investigation into Natural Language and the Sorites Paradox* (Dordrecht, The Netherlands: Kluwer, 1991).

19. On resources see H. H. Gerth and C. Wright Mills, eds., *From Max Weber: Essays in Sociology* (New York: Oxford University Press, 1958), pp. 80–81; Amitai Etzioni, *A Comparative Analysis of Complex Organizations* (New York: Free Press, 1975).

20. Arnold Toynbee, *A Study of History* (New York: Weathervane, 1972), p. 288.

21. Some of these transportation networks are discussed and/or illustrated in Richard J. A. Talbert, ed., *Atlas of Classical History* (London: Routledge, 1985), pp. 51–53, 124–27; Martin Gilbert, *Soviet History Atlas* (London: Routledge and Kegan Paul, 1979), pp. 35–36; Paul Robert Magocsi, *Historical Atlas of East-Central Europe* (Seattle: University of Washington Press, 1993), pp. 90–92; John Haywood, *Atlas of World History* (New York: Barnes and Noble, 1997). See also Michael Mann, *The Sources of Social Power: A History of Power from the Beginning to A.D. 1760*, vol. 1 (Cambridge: Cambridge University Press, 1986), pp. 275–77; Meinig, *Shaping of America*, vol. 1, pp. 65–76.

22. On totalitarianism see Alexander J. Motyl, "The End of Sovietology: From Soviet Studies to Post-Soviet Studies," in Alexander J. Motyl, ed., *The Post-Soviet Nations: Perspectives on the Demise of the USSR*, pp. 302–14 (New York: Columbia University Press, 1992).

23. David A. Lake, "The Rise, Fall, and Future of the Russian Empire," in Dawisha and Parrott, *The End of Empire?* p. 35.

24. On the differences between hegemonic, formal, and informal types of rule, see Doyle, *Empires*, pp. 34–45.

25. John Darwin, *The End of the British Empire: The Historical Debate* (Oxford: Basil Blackwell, 1991), p. 4.

26. S. N. Eisenstadt, *The Political Systems of Empires* (Glencoe, N.Y.: Free Press, 1963). See also Anton Bebler and Jim Seroka, eds., *Contemporary Political Systems: Classifications and Typologies* (Boulder, Colo.: Rienner, 1990).

27. Scholars have a large degree of agreement about the defining characteristics of empires. Ronald Suny defines empire as a "particular form of domination or control, between two units set apart in a hierarchical, inequitable relationship." Michael Doyle suggests that "empire . . . is a relationship, formal or informal, in which one state controls the effective political sovereignty of another political society." George Lichtheim defines empire as the "relationship of a hegemonial state to peoples or nations under its control." S. N. Eisenstadt notes that "the basic center-periphery relations that developed in the tsarist empire were characterized—in common with those of many other historical empires—by the differentiation, specification and crystallization of centers in general and of political centers in particular, as autonomous, structurally and symbolically

distinct entities." David Lake suggests that "in empire, one partner cedes substantial rights of residual control directly to the other; in this way, the two polities are melded together in a political relationship in which one partner controls the other." Geir Lundestad states that "empire simply means a hierarchical system of political relationships with one power being much stronger than any other." Finally, Alexander Wendt and Daniel Friedheim claim that "informal empires are structures of transnational political authority that combine an egalitarian principle of de jure sovereignty with a hierarchical principle of de facto control." See Ronald Grigor Suny, "The Empire Strikes Out: Russia, the Soviet Union, and Theories of Empire," paper prepared for "Empires and Nations: The Soviet Union and the Non-Russian Peoples," conference, University of Chicago, October 24–26, 1997, p. 5; Doyle, *Empires*, p. 45; George Lichtheim, *Imperialism* (New York: Praeger, 1971), p. 5; S. N. Eisenstadt, "Center-Periphery Relations in the Soviet Empire," in Alexander J. Motyl, ed., *Thinking Theoretically About Soviet Nationalities: History and Comparison in the Study of the USSR* (New York: Columbia University Press, 1992), p. 206; Lake, "Rise, Fall, and Future," p. 34; Geir Lundestad, *The American "Empire"* (Oslo: Norwegian University Press, 1990), p. 37; Alexander Wendt and Daniel Friedheim, "Hierarchy Under Anarchy: Informal Empire and the East German State," *International Organization* 49 (autumn 1995): 695.

28. See Niklas Luhmann, *Soziale Systeme: Grundriss einer allgemeinen Theorie* (Frankfurt am Main: Suhrkamp, 1984), pp. 30–52.

29. The work of Ferdinand de Saussure is of course critical to the notion of languages as systems.

30. Robert Jervis, *System Effects: Complexity in Political and Social Life* (Princeton, N.J.: Princeton University Press, 1997).

31. Immanuel Wallerstein, *The Modern World System*, vols. 1–2 (New York: Academic, 1974, 1979); James Rosenau, *Turbulence in World Politics: A Theory of Change and Continuity* (Princeton, N.J.: Princeton University Press, 1990).

32. Talcott Parsons, *Societies: Evolutionary and Comparative* (Englewood Cliffs, N.J.: Prentice-Hall, 1966); Luhmann, *Soziale Systeme*; Claude Lévi-Strauss, *Structural Anthropology* (New York: Basic, 1963); David Easton, *A Framework for Political Analysis* (Englewood Cliffs, N.J.: Prentice-Hall, 1965); Easton, *A Systems Analysis of Political Life* (New York: Wiley, 1965). For an excellent overview of structuralist thinking, see Jonathan Culler, *Structuralist Poetics: Structuralism, Linguistics, and the Study of Literature* (Ithaca, N.Y.: Cornell University Press, 1975). See also Giovanni Sartori, "Concept Misformation in Comparative Politics," *American Political Science Review* 64 (December 1970): 1033–53.

33. Rosenau, *Turbulence in World Politics*, pp. 49–50; Luhmann, *Soziale Systeme*, pp. 35–36.

34. For criticisms of systems theorizing, see Ronald Chilcote, *Theories of Comparative Politics: The Search for a Paradigm* (Boulder, Colo.: Westview, 1981), pp. 161–62; Malcolm Waters, *Modern Sociological Theory* (London: Sage, 1994), pp. 131–72.

35. On human irrationality see Karen Schweers Cook and Margaret Levi, eds., *The Limits of Rationality* (Chicago: University of Chicago Press, 1990); Kolja Rudzio, "Verflixte Psyche," *Die Zeit*, October 7, 1999, p. 31.

36. S. N. Eisenstadt, introduction to S. N. Eisenstadt, ed., *The Decline of Empires* (Englewood Cliffs, N.J.: Prentice-Hall, 1967), p. 1.

37. See Murray Forsyth, ed., *Federalism and Nationalism* (New York: St. Martin's, 1989).

38. Edward N. Luttwak, *The Grand Strategy of the Roman Empire* (Baltimore, Md.: Johns Hopkins University Press, 1976), pp. 80–84. See also Stephen L. Dyson, *The Creation of the Roman Frontier* (Princeton, N.J.: Princeton University Press, 1985).

39. Frantz Fanon, *The Wretched of the Earth* (New York: Grove, 1977); Albert Memmi, *The Colonizer and the Colonized* (Boston: Beacon, 1967).

40. Miles, "Roman and Modern Imperialism," p. 643.

41. Ibid., p. 647.

42. Jervis, *System Effects*, pp. 76–87.

43. Ibid., pp. 177–91.

44. Luhmann, *Soziale Systeme*, p. 382.

45. David Easton, *The Analysis of Political Structure* (New York: Routledge, 1990), pp. 273–79.

46. See Luhmann, *Soziale Systeme*, p. 384.

47. Kenneth Waltz, *Theory of International Relations* (New York: Random House, 1978), pp. 170–76.

48. Janet L. Abu-Lughod, *Before European Hegemony: The World System, A.D. 1250–1350* (New York: Oxford University Press, 1989), p. 368.

49. Robert C. Tucker, ed., *The Marx-Engels Reader*, 2d ed. (New York: Norton, 1978), p. 438.

50. Barrington Moore Jr., *Social Origins of Dictatorship and Democracy* (Boston: Beacon, 1966).

51. *Plato's Republic* (Indianapolis, Ind.: Hackett, 1974), p. 196.

52. Ibid., p. 198.

53. Mark Hagopian, *The Phenomenon of Revolution* (New York: Harper and Row, 1974).

54. Chalmers Johnson, *Revolutionary Change* (Palo Alto, Calif.: Stanford University Press, 1982); Theda Skocpol, *States and Social Revolutions* (Cambridge:

Cambridge University Press, 1979); Joseph Tainter, *The Collapse of Complex Societies* (Cambridge: Cambridge University Press, 1988); Fanon, *Wretched of the Earth*, pp. 37–39.

55. Ekkart Zimmermann, *Political Violence, Crises, and Revolutions: Theories and Research* (Boston: G. K. Hall, 1983); Martin Jänicke, ed., *Herrschaft und Krise* (Opladen, Germany: Westdeutscher Verlag, 1973).

56. Tucker, *The Marx-Engels Reader*, p. 438; Johnson, *Revolutionary Change*, p. 94; Skocpol, *States and Social Revolutions*, pp. 30–31; Tainter, *Collapse of Complex Societies*, p. 120; Fanon, *Wretched of the Earth*, p. 71.

57. Robert A. Kann, *The Habsburg Empire: A Study in Integration and Disintegration* (New York: Praeger, 1957), p. 134.

58. Cho-yun Hsu, "Roles of the Literati," p. 189.

59. Carlo M. Cipolla, introduction to Carlo M. Cipolla, ed., *The Economic Decline of Empires* (London: Methuen, 1970), p. 2. See also "Menschen machen Katastrophen," interview of Wolf Dombrowsky, *Die Zeit*, August 26, 1999, p. 15.

60. See Colin Renfrew, "Systems Collapse as Social Transformation: Catastrophe and Anastrophe in Early State Societies," in Colin Renfrew and Kenneth L. Cooke, eds., *Transformations: Mathematical Approaches to Culture Change*, pp. 481–505 (New York: Academic, 1979).

61. Herbert Kaufman, "The Collapse of Ancient States and Civilizations as an Organizational Problem," in Yoffee and Cowgill, *Collapse of Ancient States and Civilizations*, pp. 233–35; Niccolo Machiavelli, *The Prince and the Discourses* (New York: Modern Library, 1950), pp. 91–93. See also Edward Hallett Carr, *What Is History?* (New York: Vintage, 1961), pp. 130–34.

62. James D. Fearon, "Causes and Counterfactuals in Social Science: Exploring an Analogy Between Cellular Automata and Historical Processes," in Philip E. Tetlock and Aaron Belkin, eds., *Counterfactual Thought Experiments in World Politics*, pp. 39–67 (Princeton, N.J.: Princeton University Press, 1996). See also Manus I. Midlarsky, *The Disintegration of Political Systems: War and Revolution in Comparative Perspective* (Columbia: University of South Carolina Press, 1986).

63. Charles F. Doran, "Why Forecasts Fail: The Limits and Potential of Forecasting in International Relations and Economics," *International Studies Review* 1 (1999): 11.

64. See Stephen Jay Gould, *The Panda's Thumb: More Reflections in Natural History* (New York: Norton, 1980), pp. 179–93.

65. George Soros, *The Crisis of Global Capitalism: Open Society Endangered* (New York: Public Affairs, 1998).

66. William McNeill, *Plagues and Peoples* (Garden City, N.Y.: Anchor, 1976).

67. Brian Fagan, *Floods, Famines, and Empires: El Niño and the Fate of Civilizations* (New York: Basic, 1999). See also "The Big Heat," *Economist*, August 28, 1999, p. 64.

68. Sidney Hook, *The Hero in History* (Boston: Beacon, 1955), p. 203.

69. Alexander Rabinowitch, *The Bolsheviks Come to Power: The Revolution of 1917 in Petrograd* (New York: Norton, 1976), pp. 202–6.

70. Robert G. Wesson, *The Imperial Order* (Berkeley: University of California Press, 1967), p. 36.

71. Ibid., p. 334.

72. Good examples of self-contradictory arguments that try to marry choice to situations of manifest nonchoice are Steven L. Solnick, "The Breakdown of Hierarchies in the Soviet Union and China: A Neoinstitutional Perspective," *World Politics* 48 (January 1996): 209–38; James D. Fearon and David D. Laitin, "Explaining Interethnic Cooperation," *American Political Science Review* 90 (December 1996): 715–35.

73. See Imre Lakatos, "Falsification and the Methodology of Scientific Research Programmes," in Imre Lakatos and Alan Musgrave, eds., *Criticism and the Growth of Knowledge*, pp. 91–196 (Cambridge: Cambridge University Press, 1970); Stephen Gaukroger, *Explanatory Structures* (Hassocks, U.K.: Harvester, 1978).

74. Anthony Giddens, *The Constitution of Society: Outline of the Theory of Structuration* (Cambridge, U.K.: Polity, 1984).

75. See Robert A. Denemark, "World Systems History: From Traditional International Politics to the Study of Global Relations," *International Studies Review* 1 (1999): 69; Michael Taylor, "Structure, Culture, and Action in the Explanation of Social Change," *Politics and Society* 17 (June 1989): 115–62; Roger Petersen, "Mechanisms and Structures in Comparison," in John Bowen and Roger Petersen, eds., *Critical Comparisons in Politics and Culture*, pp. 61–77 (Cambridge: Cambridge University Press, 1999).

76. Arthur Danto, *Narration and Knowledge* (New York: Columbia University Press, 1985), pp. 257–84.

77. This is not to say that values have no place in social science. Quite the contrary. But they cannot serve as the sole justification for the validity of some theory. Choice is, of course, essential to questions of morality.

78. Gabriel A. Almond, *A Discipline Divided: Schools and Sects in Political Science* (Newbury Park, Calif.: Sage, 1990), pp. 51–53, 117–35.

79. Jack A. Goldstone, *Revolution and Rebellion in the Early Modern World* (Berkeley: University of California Press, 1991); Jack A. Goldstone, "Ideology, Cultural Frameworks, and the Process of Revolution," *Theory and Society* 20 (August 1991): 405–53; Skocpol, *States and Social Revolutions*; Nikki Keddie, "Can Revolutions Be Predicted; Can Their Causes Be Understood?" in Nikki

Keddie, ed., *Debating Revolutions*, pp. 3–26 (New York: New York University Press, 1995); Said Amir Arjomand, "Iran's Islamic Revolution in Comparative Perspective," *World Politics* 38 (April 1986): 383–414.

80. See Bob Sutcliffe, *Imperialism* (New York: St. Martin's, 1999).

81. See Doyle, *Empires*, pp. 19–34; Wolfgang J. Mommsen, *Theories of Imperialism* (New York: Random House, 1980).

82. Yale H. Ferguson and Richard W. Mansbach, "Global Politics at the Turn of the Millenium: Changing Bases of 'Us' and 'Them,'" *International Studies Review* 1 (1999): 79.

83. Imanuel Geiss, "Great Powers and Empires: Historical Mechanisms of Their Making and Breaking," in Geir Lundestad, ed., *The Fall of Great Powers: Peace, Stability, and Legitimacy* (Oslo: Scandinavian University Press, 1994), p. 33. But, apparently, empires are war makers. See William Eckhardt, "Civilizations, Empires, and Wars," *Journal of Peace Research* 27 (1990): 9–24.

84. Reinhold Niebuhr, *The Structure of Nations and Empires* (Fairfield, N.J.: Augustus M. Kelley, 1977), p. 66.

85. Motyl, *Revolutions, Nations, Empires*, pp. 133–36.

86. See Parker, *Geopolitics of Domination*, pp. 1–9, 64–75.

87. Lundestad, *American "Empire,"* p. 55.

88. Geoffrey Parker, *The Military Revolution: Military Innovation and the Rise of the West, 1500–1800* (Cambridge: Cambridge University Press, 1988), p. 132.

89. Lake, "Rise, Fall, and Future," p. 34. See also Yale Ferguson and Richard Mansbach, *The State, Conceptual Chaos, and the Future of International Relations Theory* (Boulder, Colo.: Rienner, 1989).

90. See Robert Gilpin, *War and Change in World Politics* (Cambridge: Cambridge University Press, 1981), pp. 106–155; David Friedman, "A Theory of the Size and Shape of Nations," *Journal of Political Economy* 85 (1977): 59–77. Hendrik Spruyt offers a sophisticated version of this argument in "Explaining Imperial Decline: The Obsolescence and Dissolution of Empires in the Modern Era," paper prepared for the convention of the American Political Science Association, Washington, D. C., August 27–31, 1997. See also Robert O. Keohane, *International Politics and State Power* (Boulder, Colo.: Westview, 1989), pp. 35–66.

91. See Peter Liberman, *Does Conquest Pay?* (Princeton, N.J.: Princeton University Press, 1996).

92. D. K. Fieldhouse, *Economics and Empire, 1830–1914* (Ithaca, N.Y.: Cornell University Press, 1973), p. 464.

93. See Charles A. Kupchan, *The Vulnerability of Empire* (Ithaca, N.Y.: Cornell University Press, 1994), pp. 90–104; Jack Snyder, *Myths of Empire* (Ithaca, N.Y.: Cornell University Press, 1991), pp. 31–65.

94. Geoffrey W. Conrad and Arthur A. Demarest, *Religion and Empire: The Dynamics of Aztec and Inca Expansionism* (Cambridge: Cambridge University Press, 1984), pp. 120–21.

95. On overextension see David A. Lake, "Anarchy, Hierarchy, and the Variety of International Relations," *International Organization* 50 (winter 1996): 1–33; Ronald Findlay, "Toward a Model of Territorial Expansion and the Limits of Empire," unpublished manuscript, Columbia University, May 1994.

96. Jean-Jacques Rousseau, *The Social Contract*, in *Discourse on Political Economy* and *The Social Contract*, trans. Christopher Betts (New York: Oxford University Press, 1994).

97. The work of David Lake illustrates many of these pitfalls. On the one hand, Lake argues that "increasing hierarchy [i.e., empire] raises the costs to the dominant state of governing the subordinate power." In particular, "to gain the subordinate party's willing consent to a hierarchic relationship, the welfare losses created by these distortions must be compensated by some transfer or side payment from the dominant state—increasing the costs to the latter. As the subordinate partner's residual control declines, and the distortions increase, so must the compensation package offered by the dominant state." On the other hand, "rent-seeking," which "creates an imperialist bias in a state's foreign policy . . . distorts the economy and reduces rates of economic growth. Over time, as the distortions accumulate, the state can improve its returns by reducing rents, freeing the economy from monopoly restrictions, and stimulating growth. . . . As the state turns from seeking rents to encouraging growth, the optimal size of the political unit will contract" (Lake, "Anarchy, Hierarchy," pp. 42, 47, 50). The flaws in Lake's analysis are fourfold. First, Lake must either anthropomorphize "the state" or use semantically meaningless predicates of the form "the state can improve," "the state turns," and so on. Second, Lake is explicitly wedded to the notion of optimal size, even though his own analysis clearly suggests that this signifier is empty. Third, Lake's insistence that empire can be a dyad like any other hierarchical relationship effectively reduces empires to little more than big states. Fourth and most important is Lake's equally problematic insistence that costs and benefits affect elite choices. This proposition assumes that the trade-offs between governance costs, opportunism, rent seeking, and economic growth are knowable to elites as trade-offs—all the time, and not just when things are obviously going wrong—and that elites choose for or against empire on that basis. But if *choice* refers to identifiable points in time when alternatives are weighed and options are considered, then elites rarely if ever really choose. Like optimal size, choice is an empty signifier.

98. For a critical treatment of rational choice theory, see Donald Green and Ian Shapiro, *Pathologies of Rational Choice Theory* (New Haven, Conn.: Yale Uni-

versity Press, 1994); Jane L. Mansbridge, ed., *Beyond Self-Interest* (Chicago, Ill.: Chicago University Press, 1990). See also Jonathan Cohn, "Irrational Exuberance," *New Republic*, October 25, 1999, pp. 25–31.

99. See Gerd Roellecke, "Du hast keine Wahl, aber triff sie," *Frankfurter Allgemeine Zeitung*, July 1, 2000.

100. See Ernst Nagel, *The Structure of Science*, 2d ed. (Indianapolis, Ind.: Hackett, 1977), pp. 30–32; Motyl, *Revolutions, Nations, Empires*, pp. 8–11.

101. Motyl, *Revolutions, Nations, Empires*, pp. 131–45.

102. Charles Diehl, "The Economic Decay of Byzantium," in Cipolla, *Economic Decline of Empires*, p. 101. I make this point in "Thinking About Empire," pp. 19–29. See also Alexander Demandt, "Die Weltreiche in der Geschichte," in Alexander Demandt, ed., *Das Ende der Weltreiche: Von den Persen bis zur Sowjetunion* (Munich: Beck, 1997), pp. 223–27.

103. Fernand Braudel, *The Structures of Everyday Life: The Limits of the Possible* (New York: Harper and Row, 1981); David Hackett Fischer, *The Great Wave: Price Revolutions and the Rhythm of History* (New York: Oxford University Press, 1996); Jared Diamond, *Guns, Germs, and Steel: The Fates of Human Societies* (New York: Norton, 1997). See also Charles Tilly, *Big Structures, Large Processes, Huge Comparisons* (New York: Russell Sage, 1984).

104. Doyle, *Empires*, pp. 128–38.

105. Ibid., p. 130.

2. Imperial Decay

1. Herbert Kaufman, "The Collapse of Ancient States and Civilizations as an Organizational Problem," in Norman Yoffee and George L. Cowgill, eds., *The Collapse of Ancient States and Civilizations* (Tucson: University of Arizona Press, 1988), pp. 228–29.

2. A. H. M. Jones, "The Social, Political, and Religious Changes During the Last Period of the Roman Empire," in S. N. Eisenstadt, ed., *The Decline of Empires* (Englewood Cliffs, N. J.: Prentice-Hall, 1967), p. 69.

3. Carlo M. Cipolla, introduction to Carlo M. Cipolla, ed., *The Economic Decline of Empires* (London: Methuen, 1970), pp. 5, 6–7.

4. Cho-yun Hsu, "The Roles of the Literati and of Regionalism in the Fall of the Han Dynasty," in Yoffee and Cowgill, *Collapse of Ancient States*, p. 189.

5. Rein Taagepera: "Expansion and Contraction Patterns for Large Polities: Context for Russia," *International Studies Quarterly* 41 (1997): 475–504; Taagepera, "Size and Duration of Empires: Growth-Decline Curves, 600 B.C. to 600 A.D.,"

Social Science History 3 (October 1979): 115–38; Taagepera, "Size and Duration of Empires: Systematics of Size," *Social Science Research* 7 (1978): 108–27; Taagepera, "Size and Duration of Empires: Growth-Decline Curves, 3000 to 600 B.C.," *Social Science Research* 7 (1978): 180–96.

6. Warren Treadgold, *A History of the Byzantine State and Society* (Palo Alto, Calif.: Stanford University Press, 1997), pp. 7–8.

7. Christopher Chase-Dunn and Thomas D. Hall, *Rise and Demise: Comparing World Systems* (Boulder, Colo.: Westview, 1997), pp. 200–29.

8. Bas van Fraassen, *Laws and Symmetry* (Oxford: Clarendon, 1989).

9. Michael E. Brown, "The Causes and Regional Dimensions of Internal Conflict," in Michael E. Brown, ed., *The International Dimensions of Internal Conflict* (Cambridge, Mass.: MIT Press, 1996), pp. 576–81.

10. On "essentially contested concepts" see William Connolly, *The Terms of Political Discourse* (Lexington, Mass.: Heath, 1974).

11. Giovanni Sartori, "Totalitarianism, Model Mania, and Learning from Error," *Journal of Theoretical Politics* 5 (1993): 5–22.

12. See Hannah Arendt, *The Origins of Totalitarianism* (New York: Harcourt Brace, 1951); Hans Buchheim, *Totalitarian Rule: Its Nature and Characteristics* (Middletown, Conn.: Wesleyan University Press, 1968); Karl Dietrich Bracher, *Die totalitäre Erfahrung* (Munich: Piper, 1987); Stephen F. Cohen, *Rethinking the Soviet Experience: Politics and History Since 1917* (New York: Oxford University Press, 1985); Bartłomiej Kamiński, "The Anatomy of the Directive Capacity of the Socialist State," *Comparative Political Studies* 22 (April 1989): 66–92; Barrington Moore Jr., *Terror and Progress—USSR* (New York: Harper, 1954); Stephen E. Hanson, "Social Theory and the Post-Soviet Crisis," *Communist and Post-Communist Studies* 28 (1995): 119–30; Ian Kershaw and Moshe Lewin, eds., *Stalinism and Nazism: Dictatorships in Comparison* (Cambridge: Cambridge University Press, 1997); Ian Kershaw, *The Nazi Dictatorship: Problems and Perspectives of Interpretation*, 2d ed. (London: Edward Arnold, 1989); *"Historikerstreit"* (Munich: Piper, 1987); Norman Davies, *Europe: A History* (Oxford: Oxford University Press, 1996), pp. 945–48. For a history of the concept see Abbott Gleason, *Totalitarianism: The Inner History of the Cold War* (New York: Oxford University Press, 1995).

13. Carl J. Friedrich and Zbigniew Brzezinski, *Totalitarian Dictatorship and Autocracy* (Cambridge, Mass.: Harvard University Press, 1956).

14. Franz Neumann, *Behemoth: The Structure and Practice of National Socialism, 1933–1944* (London: Oxford University Press, 1944).

15. Alexander J. Motyl, *Revolutions, Nations, Empires: Conceptual Limits and Theoretical Possibilities* (New York: Columbia University Press, 1999), pp. 3–15.

16. Ibid, pp. 2–3.

17. Karl Deutsch, "Cracks in the Monolith: Possibilities and Patterns of Disintegration in Totalitarian Systems," in Harry Eckstein and David E. Apter, eds., *Comparative Politics: A Reader* (New York: Free Press, 1963), pp. 498–99.

18. On stability see Alexander J. Motyl, *Will the Non-Russians Rebel? State, Ethnicity, and Stability in the USSR* (Ithaca, N.Y.: Cornell University Press, 1987), pp. 1–19.

19. It is interesting to consider whether computers might not make empires, theoretically at least, infinitely sustainable. My thanks to Polly Kummel for this insight.

20. See Alexander J. Motyl, "The End of Sovietology: From Soviet Studies to Post-Soviet Studies," in Alexander J. Motyl, ed., *The Post-Soviet Nations: Perspectives on the Demise of the USSR*, pp. 302–14 (New York: Columbia University Press, 1992).

21. See Seweryn Bialer, *Stalin's Successors: Leadership, Stability, and Change in the Soviet Union* (Cambridge: Cambridge University Press, 1980).

22. Valerie Bunce, *Subversive Institutions: The Design and the Destruction of Socialism and the State* (Cambridge: Cambridge University Press, 1999), pp. 39–40.

23. See Alec Nove, *The Soviet Economy*, rev. ed. (New York: Praeger, 1967); Merle Fainsod, *How Russia Is Ruled*, rev. ed. (Cambridge, Mass.: Harvard University Press, 1967); Barrington Moore Jr., *Soviet Politics: The Dilemma of Power* (Armonk, N.Y.: Sharpe, 1950); Richard Löwenthal, "On 'Established' Communist Party Regimes," *Studies in Comparative Communism* 7 (winter 1974): 335–58; Chalmers Johnson, ed., *Change in Communist Systems* (Palo Alto, Calif.: Stanford University Press, 1970); Maria Hirszowicz, *The Bureaucratic Leviathan: A Study in the Sociology of Communism* (New York: New York University Press, 1980); Igor' Birman, *Ekonomika nedostach* (New York: Chalidze, 1983).

24. Włodzimierz Brus, *The Economics and Politics of Socialism* (London: Routledge and Kegan Paul, 1973), pp. 13–14.

25. Deutsch, "Cracks in the Monolith," pp. 498–99.

26. Ibid., p. 499.

27. Ibid., pp. 501–2.

28. Ibid., p. 502.

29. Ibid. Deutsch is hardly alone in drawing such conclusions. According to Anthony Downs, "No one can control the behavior of large organizations; any attempt to control one large organization tends to generate another; each official tends to distort the information he passes upward in the hierarchy, exaggerating those data favorable to himself and minimizing those unfavorable to himself" (Downs, *Inside Bureaucracy* [Boston: Little Brown, 1967], pp. 262, 266). Joseph Tainter concurs: "The costs of information processing show a trend

of declining marginal productivity. . . . As the size of a social group increases, the communication load increases even faster. Information processing increases in response until capacity is reached. After this point, information processing deteriorates, so that greater costs are allocated to processing that is less efficient and reliable" (Tainter, *The Collapse of Complex Societies* [Cambridge: Cambridge University Press, 1988], p. 99). For a prescient analysis of the USSR's nonviability, see Bohdan Hawrylyshyn, *Road Maps to the Future: Toward More Effective Societies* (Oxford: Pergamon, 1980).

30. Deutsch, "Cracks in the Monolith," pp. 506–7.

31. Geoffrey Parker, *The Geopolitics of Domination* (London: Routledge, 1988), pp. 149–50.

32. G. W. Bowersock, "The Dissolution of the Roman Empire," in Yoffee and Cowgill, *Collapse of Ancient States*, pp. 170–71.

33. See E. A. Thompson, *Romans and Barbarians: The Decline of the Western Empire* (Madison: University of Wisconsin Press, 1982).

34. Geir Lundestad, "The Fall of Empires: Peace, Stability, and Legitimacy," in Geir Lundestad, ed., *The Fall of Great Powers: Peace, Stability, and Legitimacy* (Oslo: Scandinavian University Press, 1994), p. 393. See also Charles Tilly, *Coercion, Capital, and European States, A.D. 900–1990* (Cambridge, U.K.: Basil Blackwell, 1990), p. 24.

35. According to Carlo Cipolla, "The fundamental fact remains that public consumption in mature empires shows a distinct tendency to rise sharply. The phenomenon is reflected in the growth of taxation. One of the remarkably common features of empires at the later stage of their development is the growing amount of wealth pumped by the State from the economy" (see his introduction to *Economic Decline of Empires*, p. 6). Robert Gilpin writes in a similar vein: "At first, because of its initial advantages over other states, the growing state tends to expand very rapidly. In time, however, the returns to expansion diminish, and the rate of expansion slows. Finally, as the marginal costs of further expansion begin to equal or exceed the marginal benefits, expansion ceases, and an equilibrium is achieved. . . . Once a society reaches the limits of its expansion, it has great difficulty in maintaining its position and arresting its eventual decline. Further, it begins to encounter marginal returns in agricultural and industrial production. Both internal and external changes increase consumption and the costs of protection and production; it begins to experience a severe fiscal crisis. The diffusion of its economic, technological, or organizational skills undercuts its comparative advantage over other societies, especially those on the periphery of the system. These rising states, on the other hand, enjoy lower costs, rising rates of return on their resources, and the advantages of backwardness. In time, the differential rates of growth of declining and rising states in the system produce a decisive redistribution of power and

result in disequilibrium in the system" (Gilpin, *War and Change in World Politics* [Cambridge: Cambridge University Press, 1991], pp. 155, 185).

36. See Alexander J. Motyl, "Thinking About Empire," in Karen Barkey and Mark von Hagen, eds., *After Empire: Multiethnic Societies and Nation Building*, pp. 19–29 (Boulder, Colo.: Westview, 1997).

37. Kaufman, "Collapse of Ancient States," pp. 221–22.

38. See Tilly, *Coercion, Capital, and European States*, pp. 192–225. John Keegan hopes that humanity may not be "doomed to make war or that the affairs of the world must ultimately be settled by violence" (Keegan, *A History of Warfare* [New York: Knopf, 1994], p. 386). John Mueller (*Retreat from Doomsday: The Obsolescence of Modern War* [New York: Basic, 1989]) and Michael Mandelbaum ("Is Major War Obsolete?" *Survival* 40 [winter 1998–1999]: 20–38) are rather more certain that wars between great powers may be obsolete. The inductive case for their argument is weak, but, even if they prove to be right, their conclusions apply only to the future and thus to future empires. With respect to past empires, therefore, we can safely take war as a given. See also David Kaiser, *Politics and War: European Conflict from Philip II to Hitler* (Cambridge, Mass.: Harvard University Press, 1990).

39. D. W. Meinig, *The Shaping of America: Atlantic America, 1492–1800*, vol. 1 (New Haven, Conn.: Yale University Press, 1986), pp. 381–85; Richard Koebner, *Empire* (New York: Grosset and Dunlop, 1965), pp. 105–93.

40. Such a view is of course premised on the assumption that all elites pursue power and therefore engage in contention. Just such an assumption underpins Charles Tilly, *From Mobilization to Revolution* (New York: Random House, 1978), and John Breuilly, *Nationalism and the State* (Manchester, U.K.: Manchester University Press, 1982). See also Charles Taylor, "Faith and Identity: Religion and Conflict in the Modern World," *Newsletter* of the Institut für die Wissenschaften vom Menschen, no. 63 (November 1998–January 1999), pp. 28–31.

41. John Darwin writes: "The British empire did not come to an end primarily because the British lost interest in it, or dictated a rapid shedding of redundant imperial commitments. On the contrary, the recognition of the necessity of progressing towards colonial self-government coexisted with an equal determination to preserve British world power" (Darwin, *The End of the British Empire: The Historical Debate* [Oxford: Basil Blackwell, 1991], p. 114).

42. Bernard Porter, "Die Transformation des *British Empire*," in Alexander Demandt, ed., *Das Ende der Weltreiche: Von den Persern bis zur Sowjetunion* (Munich: Beck, 1997), pp. 169–71.

43. Cho-yun Hsu, "Roles of the Literati," p. 194.

44. Ibid., p. 187.

45. Ibid., p. 195.

46. Ibid., pp. 191, 193.

47. Ibid., pp. 194–95. See also Chase-Dunn and Hall, *Rise and Demise*, pp. 158–63.

48. Michael W. Doyle, *Empires* (Ithaca, N.Y.: Cornell University Press, 1986), pp. 101–2. See also Helmuth Schneider, "Das Ende des Imperium Romanum im Westen," in Richard Lorenz, ed., *Das Verdämmern der Macht: Vom Untergang grosser Reiche* (Frankfurt am Main: Fischer Taschenbuch Verlag, 2000), p. 31.

49. Alexander Demandt, "Die Auflösung des römischen Reiches," in Demandt, *Das Ende der Weltreiche*, p. 40.

50. Peter Garnsey and Richard Saller, *The Roman Empire: Economy, Society, and Culture* (Berkeley: University of California Press, 1987), p. 20.

51. Philippe Contamine, *War in the Middle Ages* (Oxford: Basil Blackwell, 1984), p. 9.

52. Arther Ferrill, *The Fall of the Roman Empire* (London: Thames and Hudson, 1986).

53. Bernard Lewis, "Some Reflections on the Decline of the Ottoman Empire," in Cipolla, *Economic Decline of Empires*, p. 217.

54. Ibid., p. 228.

55. Engin D. Akarli, "Economic Policy and Budgets in Ottoman Turkey, 1876–1909," *Middle Eastern Studies* 28 (July 1992): 446, 466–467. See also Donald Quataert, *Social Disintegration and Popular Resistance in the Ottoman Empire, 1881–1908* (New York: New York University Press, 1983).

56. Akarli, "Economic Policy and Budgets," p. 448.

57. Carter V. Findley, *Bureaucratic Reform in the Ottoman Empire: The Sublime Porte, 1789–1922* (Princeton, N.J.: Princeton University Press, 1980), pp. 337–47.

58. Akarli, "Economic Policy and Budgets," p. 460.

59. Geoffrey Parker, *The Military Revolution: Military Innovation and the Rise of the West, 1500–1800* (Cambridge: Cambridge University Press, 1988), pp. 126–28.

60. Bernard Lewis, *The Emergence of Modern Turkey*, 2d ed. (London: Oxford University Press, 1968); Benjamin Miller and Korina Kagan, "The Great Powers and Regional Conflicts: Eastern Europe and the Balkans from the Post-Napoleonic Era to the Post–Cold War Era," *International Studies Quarterly* 41 (1997): 51–85.

61. Treadgold, *History of the Byzantine State and Society*, p. 677. See Franz Georg Maier's discussion of *Pronoia* in "Byzanz: Selbstbehauptung und Zerfall einer Grossmacht," in Lorenz, *Das Verdämmern der Macht*, pp. 53–54.

62. George Ostrogorsky, *History of the Byzantine State* (New Brunswick, N.J.: Rutgers University Press, 1969), p. 323.

63. Ibid., p. 481.
64. Charles Diehl, "The Economic Decay of Byzantium," in Cipolla, *Economic Decline of Empires*, p. 100.
65. Maier, "Byzanz," p. 49.
66. Treadgold, *History of the Byzantine State and Society*, p. 813.
67. Ostrogorsky, *History of the Byzantine State*, pp. 499–533; Archibald R. Lewis, *Nomads and Crusaders, A.D. 1000–1368* (Bloomington: Indiana University Press, 1988), pp. 154–55, 192–93.
68. Doyle, *Empires*, p. 120.
69. Ibid., p. 102.
70. Renate Pieper, "Des Ende des Spanischen Kolonialreiches in Amerika," in Demandt, *Das Ende der Weltreiche*, p. 79.
71. Hans-Joachim König, "Der Zerfall des Spanischen Weltreichs in Amerika: Ursachen und Folgen," in Lorenz, *Das Verdämmern der Macht*, p. 145.
72. Doyle, *Empires*, pp. 331–35; König, "Der Zerfall des Spanischen Weltreichs," p. 147.
73. Franz Ansprenger, *The Dissolution of the Colonial Empires* (London: Routledge, 1989), pp. 266–89.
74. Eric J. Hobsbawm, *Industry and Empire: From 1750 to the Present Day* (London: Penguin, 1968), pp. 218–21 (see p. 218 for the quote); see also Paul Kennedy, *The Rise and Fall of the Great Powers* (New York: Vintage, 1987), pp. 275–91.
75. Kennedy, *Rise and Fall of the Great Powers*, pp. 347–72. See especially Roland Höhne, "Die Auflösung des französischen Kolonialreiches, 1946–1962," in Lorenz, *Das Verdämmern der Macht*, pp. 205–35.
76. Darwin, *End of the British Empire*, p. 120. See also Horst Dippel, "Die Auflösung des Britischen Empire oder die Suche nach einem Reichersatz für formale Herrschaft," in Lorenz, *Das Verdämmern der Macht*, p. 252.
77. Michael Graham Fry, "Colonization: Britain, France, and the Cold War," in Karen Dawisha and Bruce Parrott, eds., *The End of Empire? The Transformation of the USSR in Comparative Perspective* (Armonk, N.Y.: Sharpe, 1997), pp. 128–35.
78. Kennedy, *Rise and Fall*, p. 366.
79. Tilly, *Coercion, Capital, and European States*, p. 198.
80. Ansprenger, *Dissolution of the Colonial Empires*, pp. 159–207; Fry, "Colonization," pp. 138–45.
81. Tainter, *Collapse of Complex Societies*, p. 127.
82. Cipolla, introduction to *Economic Decline of Empires*, pp. 13–14.
83. Ibid., pp. 7–13.
84. David Good's analysis of the late Habsburg economy shows that economic growth can occur in mature empires if states withdraw from the economy

(Good, *The Economic Rise of the Habsburg Empire, 1750–1914* [Berkeley: University of California Press, 1984]). See also William R. Thompson, "Long Waves, Technological Innovation, and Relative Decline," *International Organization* 44 (spring 1990): 202–7.

85. Tainter, *Collapse of Complex Societies*, pp. 99–106.
86. Paul Claval, "Centre/Periphery and Space: Models of Political Geography," in Jean Gottmann, ed., *Centre and Periphery: Spatial Variation in Politics*, pp. 63–71 (Beverly Hills, Calif.: Sage, 1980).

3. Imperial Collapse

1. Richard Lorenz, "Das Ender der Sowjetunion," in Richard Lorenz, ed., *Das Verdämmern der Macht: Vom Untergang grosser Reiche* (Frankfurt am Main: Fischer Taschenbuch Verlag, 2000), p. 278.
2. Seweryn Bialer, *Stalin's Successors: Leadership, Stability, and Change in the Soviet Union* (Cambridge: Cambridge University Press, 1980); Ed A. Hewett, *Reforming the Soviet Economy* (Washington, D.C.: Brookings Institution, 1988); James R. Millar, *The ABCs of Soviet Socialism* (Urbana: University of Illinois Press, 1981).
3. János Kornai, *The Socialist System: The Political Economy of Communism* (Princeton, N.J.: Princeton University Press, 1992); Richard E. Ericson, "Soviet Economic Structure and the National Question," in Alexander J. Motyl, ed., *The Post-Soviet Nations: Perspectives on the Demise of the USSR*, pp. 240–71 (New York: Columbia University Press, 1992); Igor' Birman, *Ekonomika nedostach* (New York: Chalidze, 1983).
4. Ronald Grigor Suny, *Revenge of the Past* (Palo Alto, Calif.: Stanford University Press, 1993); Bruce Parrott, "Analyzing the Transformation of the Soviet Union in Comparative Perspective," in Karen Dawisha and Bruce Parrott, eds., *The End of Empire? The Transformation of the USSR in Comparative Perspective*, pp. 3–29 (Armonk, N.Y.: Sharpe, 1997); Hélène Carrère d'Encausse, *Decline of an Empire: The Soviet Socialist Republics in Revolt* (New York: Newsweek Books, 1979).
5. Timothy Garton Ash, "The Empire in Decay," *New York Review of Books*, September 29, 1988, p. 56.
6. Joseph Rothschild, *The Return to Diversity* (Oxford: Oxford University Press, 1989); Rudolf Tőkés, ed., *Opposition in Eastern Europe* (Baltimore, Md.: Johns Hopkins University Press, 1979); Elemér Hankiss, *East European Alternatives* (Oxford: Clarendon, 1990); Teresa Rakowska-Harmstone and Andrew Gyorgy, eds., *Communism in Eastern Europe* (Bloomington: Indiana Univer-

sity Press, 1979); Rey Koslowski and Friedrich V. Kratochwil, "Understanding Change in International Politics: The Soviet Empire's Demise and the International System," *International Organization* 48 (spring 1994): 235–41; Zdeněk Mlynář, *Krisen und Krisenbewältigung in Sowjetblock* (Vienna: Bund-Verlag and Braumüller, 1983).

7. Stephen M. Meyer, "The Military," in Timothy J. Colton and Robert Legvold, eds., *After the Soviet Union: From Empire to Nations* (New York: Norton, 1992), p. 113. See also William E. Odom, *The Collapse of the Soviet Military* (New Haven, Conn.: Yale University Press, 1998).

8. Seweryn Bialer, *The Soviet Paradox: External Expansion, Internal Decline* (New York: Knopf, 1986).

9. Paul Robert Magocsi, *Historical Atlas of East-Central Europe* (Seattle: University of Washington Press, 1993), pp. 73–75.

10. Robert Kann, *The Habsburg Empire: A Study in Integration and Disintegration* (New York: Praeger, 1957), pp. 25–37.

11. Robert Kann, *A History of the Habsburg Empire, 1526–1918* (Berkeley: University of California Press, 1974).

12. Kann, *The Habsburg Empire*, p. 10.

13. A. J. P. Taylor, *The Habsburg Monarchy, 1809–1918* (Chicago: University of Chicago Press, 1948), pp. 123–40.

14. Alan Sked, *The Decline and Fall of the Habsburg Empire, 1815–1918* (London: Longman, 1989), pp. 192–93.

15. Istvan Deak, "The Fall of Austria-Hungary: Peace, Stability, and Legitimacy," in Geir Lundestad, ed., *The Fall of Great Powers: Peace, Stability, and Legitimacy* (Oslo: Scandinavian University Press, 1994), p. 85.

16. Peter F. Sugar, "The Nature of the Non-Germanic Societies Under Habsburg Rule," *Slavic Review* 22 (March 1963): 1–30.

17. Frederick Engels, *Germany: Revolution and Counterrevolution* (New York: International, 1969). See also Barbara Jelavich, *The Habsburg Empire in European Affairs, 1814–1918* (Chicago: Rand McNally, 1969), pp. 57–68.

18. Paul Kennedy, *The Rise and Fall of the Great Powers* (New York: Vintage, 1987), pp. 217–19.

19. Deak, "Fall of Austria-Hungary," pp. 89–90.

20. Istvan Deak, *Beyond Nationalism: A Social and Political History of the Habsburg Officer Corps, 1848–1918* (Oxford: Oxford University Press, 1990).

21. Edward C. Thaden, *Russia's Western Borderlands, 1710–1870* (Princeton, N.J.: Princeton University Press, 1984).

22. Marc Raeff, *Understanding Imperial Russia* (New York: Columbia University Press, 1984), pp. 36–37.

23. Ronald Grigor Suny, *The Making of the Georgian Nation* (Bloomington: Indiana University Press, 1988); Edward Allworth, ed., *Central Asia: A Century*

of Russian Rule (New York: Columbia University Press, 1967); John A. Armstrong, "Mobilized Diaspora in Tsarist Russia: The Case of the Baltic Germans," in Jeremy Azrael, ed., *Soviet Nationality Policies and Practices*, pp. 63–104 (New York: Praeger, 1978); Ronald Grigor Suny, ed., *Transcaucasia: Nationalism and Social Change* (Ann Arbor: University of Michigan Press, 1983); Seymour Becker, *Russia's Protectorates in Central Asia: Bukhara and Khiva, 1865–1924* (Cambridge, Mass.: Harvard University Press, 1968).

24. Martin C. Spechler, "Economic Advantages of Being Peripheral: Subordinate Nations in Multinational Empires," unpublished manuscript, University of Indiana. See also Erkki Pihkala, "Der baltische Handel Finnlands, 1835–1944," *Jahrbücher für Geschichte Osteuropas* 23 (1975): 1–25.

25. Walter M. Pinter, "The Burden of Defense in Imperial Russia, 1725–1914," *Russian Review* 43 (1984): 249, 242, 245. See also John L. H. Keep, "The Russian Army's Response to the French Revolution," *Jahrbücher für Geschichte Osteuropas* 28 (1980): 500–23.

26. Kennedy, *Rise and Fall of the Great Powers*, pp. 236–40.

27. See also Joseph Tainter, *The Collapse of Complex Societies* (Cambridge: Cambridge University Press, 1988), p. 124.

28. A. H. M. Jones, "The Social, Political, and Religious Changes During the Last Period of the Roman Empire," in S. N. Eisenstadt, ed., *The Decline of Empires* (Englewood Cliffs, N.J.: Prentice-Hall, 1967), pp. 159–60.

29. See Merle Fainsod, *How Russia Is Ruled*, rev. ed. (Cambridge, Mass.: Harvard University Press, 1967); Jerry F. Hough and Merle Fainsod, *How the Soviet Union Is Governed* (Cambridge, Mass.: Harvard University Press, 1979); Barrington Moore Jr., *Soviet Politics: The Dilemma of Power* (Armonk, N.Y.: Sharpe, 1950).

30. Solomon Wank, "The Disintegration of the Habsburg and Ottoman Empires: A Comparative Analysis," in Dawisha and Parrott, *End of Empire?* p. 112.

31. Ibid., pp. 110–11.

32. Kann, *The Habsburg Empire*, p. 154.

33. See Charles A. Kupchan, *The Vulnerability of Empire* (Ithaca, N.Y.: Cornell University Press, 1994), pp. 33–104.

34. Samuel R. Williamson Jr., *Austria-Hungary and the Origins of the First World War* (Houndmills, U.K.: Macmillan, 1991), p. 215.

35. Tainter, *Collapse of Complex Societies*, pp. 124–26. See also David Hackett Fischer, *The Great Wave: Price Revolutions and the Rhythm of History* (New York: Oxford University Press, 1996), and Jahangir Amuzegar, "OPEC as Omen," *Foreign Affairs* 77 (November–December 1998): 95–111.

36. See Henry Munson Jr., *Islam and Revolution in the Middle East* (New Haven, Conn.: Yale University Press, 1988), pp. 11–12.

37. Fischer, *Great Wave*, pp. 82–83.

38. Leslie Dienes, *Soviet Asia: Economic Development and National Policy Choices* (Boulder, Colo.: Westview, 1987).

39. Bernard Lewis, *The Emergence of Modern Turkey*, 2d ed. (Oxford: Oxford University Press, 1968).

40. Henri Pirenne, *Mohammed and Charlemagne* (London: Allen and Unwin, 1939). See also Immanuel Wallerstein, *The Modern World System: Capitalist Agriculture and the Origins of the European World Economy in the Sixteenth Century* (New York: Academic, 1976); Immanuel Wallerstein, *The Modern World System II: Mercantilism and the Consolidation of the European World Economy, 1600–1750* (New York: Academic Press, 1980); Janet L. Abu-Lughod, *Before European Hegemony: The World System, A.D. 1250–1350* (New York: Oxford University Press, 1989).

41. John Noble Wilford, "Collapse of Earliest Known Empire Is Linked to Long, Harsh Drought," *New York Times*, August 24, 1993, pp. C1, C10; William H. McNeill, *Plagues and Peoples* (Garden City, N.Y.: Anchor, 1976), pp. 175–85.

42. Geoffrey W. Conrad and Arthur A. Demarest, *Religion and Empire: The Dynamics of Aztec and Inca Expansionism* (Cambridge: Cambridge University Press, 1984), p. 69.

43. Brian Fagan, *Floods, Famines, and Empires: El Niño and the Fate of Civilizations* (New York: Basic, 1999), p. xvi.

44. See Douglas Hofstadter, *Gödel, Escher, Bach* (New York: Vintage, 1989); Richard Boyd, Philip Gasper, and J. D. Trout, eds., *The Philosophy of Science* (Cambridge, Mass.: MIT Press, 1991).

45. Ehrhard Behrens, "'P = NP?': Oder, Anders Gefragt: Ist Glück in der Mathematik entbehrlich?" *Die Zeit*, March 4, 1999, p. 43.

46. James Rosenau, *Turbulence in World Politics: A Theory of Change and Continuity* (Princeton, N.J.: Princeton University Press, 1990), p. 90.

47. Fagan, *Floods, Famines, and Empires*, p. 51.

48. Tainter, *Collapse of Complex Societies*, p. 127. Although most of his themes will find their way individually into my argument, on the whole Tainter's scheme is of limited utility to a study of empires in general and imperial collapse in particular. First, his unit of analysis is "society" and not any particular polity or political ordering thereof. Second, Tainter defines *collapse* not in terms of the society per se but in terms of complexity: "A society has collapsed when it displays a rapid, significant loss of an established level of sociopolitical complexity" (p. 4). Because society and complexity are almost synonymous for Tainter, it follows that the collapse of either, or of both, is possible only "in a power vacuum . . . when there is no competitor strong enough to fill the political vacuum of disintegration" (p. 202). Finally, Tainter's view of both

collapse and complexity is much too broad to accommodate my own, far narrower focus on mere empires as peculiar kinds of political systems. One immediate consequence of this difference in perspectives is that the Habsburg empire could not on his account really have collapsed, as its complex society was merely redivided, while for me it decidedly did.

49. Theda Skocpol, *States and Social Revolutions* (Cambridge: Cambridge University Press, 1979).

50. Robert Gilpin, *War and Change in World Politics* (Cambridge: Cambridge University Press, 1981).

51. A. B. Bosworth, *Conquest and Empire: The Reign of Alexander the Great* (Cambridge: Cambridge University Press, 1988), p. 174.

52. On crisis see James O'Connor, *The Meaning of Crisis* (Oxford: Basil Blackwell, 1987); Alexander J. Motyl, "Reassessing the Soviet Crisis: Big Problems, Muddling Through, Business as Usual," *Political Science Quarterly* 104 (summer 1989): 269–80.

53. Kennedy, *Rise and Fall of the Great Powers*, pp. 232–41.

54. Alexander J. Motyl, *Sovietology, Rationality, Nationality: Coming to Grips with Nationalism in the USSR* (New York: Columbia University Press, 1990), pp. 103–18.

55. Richard Pipes, *The Formation of the Soviet Union* (New York: Atheneum, 1974).

56. Geoffrey Parker, *The Geopolitics of Domination* (London: Routledge, 1988), pp. 76–99.

57. Kennedy, *Rise and Fall of the Great Powers*, pp. 209–15.

58. Hans-Ulrich Wehler, *The German Empire, 1871–1918* (Dover, N.H.: Berg, 1985), pp. 42–44.

59. Kennedy, *Rise and Fall of the Great Powers*, pp. 268–74; Wehler, *German Empire*, pp. 201–9.

60. David Stevenson, *The First World War and International Politics* (Oxford: Clarendon, 1988), pp. 230–31; Alan Sharp, *The Versailles Settlement: Peacemaking in Paris, 1919* (New York: St. Martin's, 1991), pp. 102–29.

61. Wank, "Disintegration of the Habsburg and Ottoman Empires," p. 111.

62. Ibid., pp. 110–11.

63. Ibid., pp. 110–13.

64. Bialer, *Stalin's Successors* and *The Soviet Paradox*.

65. Gerhard Simon, "Die Disintegration der Sowjetunion," in Alexander Demandt, ed., *Das Ende der Weltreiche: Von den Persen bis zur Sowjetunion*, pp. 174–210 (Munich: Beck, 1997); Motyl, *Sovietology, Rationality, Nationality* pp. 59–71.

66. Reneo Lukic and Allen Lynch, *Europe from the Balkans to the Urals: The Disintegration of Yugoslavia and the Soviet Union* (Oxford: Oxford University Press, 1996), p. 383.

67. Alexander J. Motyl, "Totalitarian Collapse, Imperial Disintegration, and the Rise of the Soviet West," in Michael Mandelbaum, ed., *The Rise of Nations in the Soviet Union: American Foreign Policy and the Disintegration of the USSR*, pp. 44–63 (New York: Council on Foreign Relations, 1991); Alexander J. Motyl, "Empire or Stability? The Case for Soviet Dissolution," *World Policy Journal* 8 (summer 1991): 499–524.

68. Valerie Bunce, *Subversive Institutions: The Design and the Destruction of Socialism and the State* (Cambridge: Cambridge University Press, 1999), p. 41.

69. Archie Brown, *The Gorbachev Factor* (Oxford: Oxford University Press, 1996). For a contrary view see John Armstrong, "Gorbachev: Limits of the Fox in Soviet Politics," *Soviet and Post-Soviet Review* 19 (1992): 89–97.

70. Alexander J. Motyl, "The Sobering of Gorbachev: Nationality, Restructuring, and the West," in Seweryn Bialer, ed., *Politics, Society, and Nationality Inside Gorbachev's Russia*, pp. 149–73 (Boulder, Colo.: Westview, 1989).

71. Valerie Bunce, *Do New Leaders Make a Difference? Executive Succession and Public Policy Under Capitalism and Socialism* (Princeton, N.J.: Princeton University Press, 1981); George W. Breslauer, *Khrushchev and Brezhnev as Leaders: Building Authority in Soviet Politics* (London: Allen and Unwin, 1982).

72. Kann, *The Habsburg Empire*, pp. 163–64.

73. Motyl, *Sovietology, Rationality, Nationality*, pp. 111–18.

74. Rothschild, *Return to Diversity*; Michael Bernhard, *The Origins of Democratization in Poland: Workers, Intellectuals, and Oppositional Politics, 1976–1980* (New York: Columbia University Press, 1993); Bartłomiej Kamiński, *The Collapse of State Socialism: The Case of Poland* (Princeton, N.J.: Princeton University Press, 1991); Joni Lovenduski and Jean Woodall, *Politics and Society in Eastern Europe* (Bloomington: Indiana University Press, 1987); Zbigniew Rau, ed., *The Reemergence of Civil Society in Eastern Europe and the Soviet Union* (Boulder, Colo.: Westview, 1991).

75. Romuald J. Misiunas and Rein Taagepera, *The Baltic States: Years of Dependence, 1940–1980* (Berkeley: University of California Press, 1983); Rein Taagepera, *Estonia: Return to Independence* (Boulder, Colo.: Westview, 1993); V. Stanley Vardys and Judith B. Sedaitis, *Lithuania: The Rebel Nation* (Boulder, Colo.: Westview, 1997).

76. See Motyl, *Post-Soviet Nations*; Alexander J. Motyl, ed., *Thinking Theoretically About Soviet Nationalities: History and Comparison in the Study of the USSR* (New York: Columbia University Press, 1992).

77. Raimondo Strassoldo, "Centre-Periphery and System-Boundary: Culturological Perspectives," in Jean Gottmann, ed., *Centre and Periphery: Spatial Variations in Politics* (Beverly Hills, Calif.: Sage, 1980), p. 45.

78. Motyl, "Reassessing the Soviet Crisis."

4. Imperial Revival

1. In Arnold Toynbee's words, "A successor state that is struggling to establish itself is seldom inhibited by political or cultural animosity from taking over from its imperial predecessor a vital administrative technique or even an existing professional personnel, in order to maintain governmental stability" (Toynbee, *A Study of History* [New York: Weathervane, 1972], p. 314).

2. On state capacity see Joel Migdal, *Strong Societies, Weak States* (Princeton, N.J.: Princeton University Press, 1988); Stephen M. Walt, *Revolution and War* (Ithaca, N.Y.: Cornell University Press, 1996), pp. 21–22; Alfred Stepan, *The State and Society: Peru in Comparative Perspective* (Princeton, N.J.: Princeton University Press, 1978); James A. Caporaso, ed., *The Elusive State: International and Comparative Perspectives* (Newbury Park, Calif.: Sage, 1989); Philip G. Cerny, *The Changing Architecture of Politics: Structure, Agency, and the Future of the State* (London: Sage, 1990).

3. See Michael Doyle, *Empires* (Ithaca, N.Y.: Cornell University Press, 1986), pp. 128–35.

4. Geir Lundestad, "The Fall of Empires: Peace, Stability, and Legitimacy," in Geir Lundestad, ed., *The Fall of Great Powers: Peace, Stability, and Legitimacy* (Oslo: Scandinavian University Press, 1994), p. 384.

5. See Ian Lustick, *Unsettled States, Disputed Lands: Britain and Ireland, France and Algeria, Israel and the West Bank–Gaza* (Ithaca, N.Y.: Cornell University Press, 1993); Alexander J. Motyl, "Reifying Boundaries, Fetishizing the Nation: Soviet Legacies and Elite Legitimacy in the Post-Soviet States," in Ian Lustick and Brendan O'Leary, eds., *Rightsizing the State* (Oxford: Oxford University Press, forthcoming).

6. Rogers Brubaker, *Nationalism Reframed* (Cambridge: Cambridge University Press, 1996).

7. Doyle, *Empires*, pp. 128–38.

8. Robert Kann, *A History of the Habsburg Empire, 1526–1918* (Berkeley: University of California Press, 1974).

9. Solomon Wank, "The Disintegration of the Habsburg and Ottoman Empires: A Comparative Analysis," in Karen Dawisha and Bruce Parrott, eds., *The End of Empire? The Transformation of the USSR in Comparative Perspective* (Armonk, N.Y.: Sharpe, 1997), p. 105.

10. Istvan Deak, "The Habsburg Empire," in Karen Barkey and Mark von Hagen, eds., *After Empire: Multiethnic Societies and Nation Building*, pp. 129–41 (Boulder, Colo.: Westview, 1997).

11. Alan Sharp, *The Versailles Settlement: Peacemaking in Paris, 1919* (New York: St. Martin's, 1991), pp. 165–84; Bernard Lewis, *The Emergence of Modern Turkey*, 2d ed. (London: Oxford University Press, 1968).

12. Andreas Kappeler, *Russland als Vielvölkerstaat* (Munich: Beck, 1992); Hugh Seton Watson, *The Decline of Imperial Russia, 1855–1914* (New York: Praeger, 1961).

13. Ewan Mawdsley, *The Russian Civil War* (Boston, Mass.: Allen and Unwin, 1987).

14. Alexander J. Motyl, *Sovietology, Rationality, Nationality: Coming to Grips with Nationalism in the USSR* (New York: Columbia University Press, 1990), pp. 116–17.

15. See Hans-Ulrich Wehler, *The German Empire, 1871–1918* (Dover, N.H.: Berg, 1985), pp. 9–51; Wolfgang J. Mommsen, *Der autoritäre Nationalstaat: Verfassung, Gesellschaft und Kultur im deutschen Kaiserreich* (Frankfurt am Main: Fischer Taschenbuch Verlag, 1990), pp. 234–56.

16. Andreas Hillgruber, "The Historical Significance of the First World War: A Seminal Catastrophe," in Gregor Schöllgen, ed., *Escape into War? The Foreign Policy of Imperial Germany* (Oxford: Berg, 1990), p. 175.

17. David Stevenson, *The First World War and International Politics* (Oxford: Clarendon, 1988), p. 310.

18. Paul Kennedy, *The Rise and Decline of the Great Powers* (New York: Vintage: 1987), pp. 275–333.

19. See Woodruff D. Smith, *The Ideological Origins of Nazi Imperialism* (New York: Oxford University Press, 1986). According to David Kaiser, "Hitler, more than any other individual in modern history, demonstrated the possible extent and the ultimate limit of the role of a single individual in international politics. Despite the experience of the First World War and the limitations upon German resources in the 1930s, which would clearly have dissuaded many other German leaders from preparing for or unleashing another general war in Europe, he managed by careful manipulation of contemporary politics, economics, and military technology to conquer most of Western Europe and to bring his armies to the banks of the Volga. . . . But he could not prevail in a long-term struggle with economically superior powers, and he could not turn to diplomacy when the military balance turned against him. His opponents in the Second World War not only blamed the war upon Hitler and the Nazi regime but also insisted upon total victory and unconditional surrender" (Smith, *Politics and War: European Conflict from Philip II to Hitler* [Cambridge, Mass.: Harvard University Press, 1990], pp. 390–91). For a discussion of the range of interpretations of Hitler's role, see Ian Kershaw, *The Nazi Dictatorship: Problems and Perspectives of Interpretation*, 2d ed. (London: Edward Arnold, 1989); Michael R. Marrus, *The Holocaust in History* (London: Weidenfeld and Nicolson, 1988).

20. I also make this point, but for other reasons, in Alexander J. Motyl, "Why Empires Reemerge: Imperial Collapse and Imperial Revival in Comparative Perspective," *Comparative Politics* 31 (January 1999): 127–45.

21. Rogers Brubaker, "Aftermaths of Empire and the Unmixing of Peoples," in Barkey and von Hagen, *After Empire*, pp. 155–80; Brubaker, *Nationalism Reframed*, pp. 117–18.

22. Alexander J. Motyl, "After Empire: Competing Discourses and Interstate Conflict in Postimperial Eastern Europe," in Barnett Rubin and Jack Snyder, eds., *Post-Soviet Political Order: Conflict and State Building*, pp. 14–33 (London: Routledge, 1998).

23. See Alexander Yanov, *Weimar Russia and What We Can Do About It* (New York: Slovo, n.d.). Zbigniew Brzezinski believes that the more appropriate comparison is between post-Soviet Russia and post-Ottoman Turkey. See his "Living with Russia," *National Interest*, no. 61 (fall 2000): 5–16.

24. Alexander J. Motyl, "Institutional Legacies and Reform Trajectories," in Adrian Karatnycky, Alexander J. Motyl, and Boris Shor, eds., *Nations in Transit, 1997*, pp. 17–22 (New Brunswick, N.J.: Transaction, 1997).

25. Alexander J. Motyl, *Revolutions, Nations, Empires: Conceptual Limits and Theoretical Possibilities* (New York: Columbia University Press, 1999), pp. 51–58.

26. Edward Allworth, ed., *Ethnic Russia in the USSR* (New York: Pergamon, 1980); S. Enders Wimbush, "The Great Russians and the Soviet State: The Dilemmas of Ethnic Dominance," in Jeremy R. Azrael, ed., *Soviet Nationality Policies and Practices*, pp. 349–60 (New York: Praeger, 1978).

27. Lilia Shevtsova and Scott A. Bruckner, "Toward Stability or Crisis?" *Journal of Democracy* 8 (January 1997): 12–26. See also Lilia Shevtsova, *Yeltsin's Russia: Myths and Reality* (Washington, D.C.: Carnegie Endowment for International Peace, 1999); Alexander J. Motyl, "Structural Constraints and Starting Points: The Logic of Systemic Change in Ukraine and Russia," *Comparative Politics* 29 (July 1997): 433–47.

28. Valerie Sperling, ed., *Building the Russian State: Institutional Crisis and the Quest for Democratic Governance* (Boulder, Colo.: Westview, 2000).

29. See Anders Åslund and Marth Brill Olcott, eds., *Russia After Communism* (Washington, D.C.: Carnegie Endowment for International Peace, 1999); Pål Kolstø, *Political Construction Sites: Nation Building in Russia and the Post-Soviet States* (Boulder, Colo.: Westview, 2000); U.S. National Intelligence Council and Bureau of Intelligence and Research, *Conference Report: Federation in Russia: How Is It Working?* (Washington, D.C.: National Intelligence Council, 1999); Dietmar Müller, *Regionalisierung des postsowjetischen Raumes* (Berlin: Osteuropa-Institut, 1997).

30. See Valentin Michajlov, "Tatarstan: Jahre der Souveränität. Eine kurze Bilanz," *Osteuropa* 49 (April 1999): 366–86; John F. Young, "The Republic of Sakha and Republic Building: The Neverendum of Federalization in Russia," in Kim-

itaka Matsuzato, ed., *Regions: A Prism to View the Slavic-Eurasian World*, pp. 177–207 (Sapporo, Japan: Slavic Research Center, Hokkaido University, 2000); Michael Rywkin, "The Autonomy of Bashkirs," *Central Asian Survey* 12 (1993): 47–57.

31. See Jack F. Matlock, "Dealing with a Russia in Turmoil," *Foreign Affairs* 75 (May–June 1996): 38–51; Sherman Garnett, "Russia's Illusory Ambitions," *Foreign Affairs* 76 (March–April 1997): 61–76; Stephen M. Meyer, "The Military," in Timothy J. Colton and Robert Legvold, eds., *After the Soviet Union: From Empire to Nations*, pp. 113–46 (New York: Norton, 1992); Anatol Lieven, *Ukraine and Russia: A Fraternal Rivalry* (Washington, D.C.: U.S. Institute of Peace, 1999); William E. Odom, *The Collapse of the Soviet Military* (New Haven, Conn.: Yale University Press, 1998).

32. See Thomas Graham and Arnold Horelick, *U.S.-Russian Relations at the Turn of the Century* (Washington, D.C.: Carnegie Endowment for International Peace, 1999).

33. Anatol Lieven, *Chechnya: Tombstone of Russian Power* (New Haven, Conn.: Yale University Press, 1998).

34. On the second Chechen war see Rajan Menon and Graham E. Fuller, "Russia's Ruinous Chechen War," *Foreign Affairs* 79 (March–April 2000): 32–44; Uwe Halbach, "Der Weg in den zweiten Tschetschenien-Krieg," *Osteuropa* 50 (January 2000): 11–30. See also Gail W. Lapidus, "Contested Sovereignty: The Tragedy of Chechnya," *International Security* 23 (summer 1998): 5–49.

35. Center for Peace, Conversion, and Foreign Policy of Ukraine, "The Armed Forces of Ukraine: Orientations of Servicemen," occasional report, October 13, 1999, Kyiv.

36. See Margarita Mercedes Balmaceda, "Gas, Oil, and the Linkages Between Domestic and Foreign Policies: The Case of Ukraine," *Europe-Asia Studies* 50 (March 1998): 257–86; Eric A. Miller and Arkady Toritsyn, "Elite Foreign Policy in the Former Soviet Union," unpublished manuscript, n.d.; Rajan Menon, Ghia Nodia, and Yuri Fyodorov, eds., *Russia, the Caucasus, and Central Asia: The Twenty-first–Century Security Environment* (Armonk, N.Y.: Sharpe, 1999); Andreas Heinrich, "Der ungeklärte Status des Kaspischen Meeres," *Osteuropa* 49 (July 1999): 671–83.

37. Rajan Menon, "In the Shadow of the Bear: Security in Post-Soviet Central Asia," *International Security* 20 (summer 1995): 149–81; Rajan Menon, "After Empire: Russia and the Southern 'Near Abroad,'" in Michael Mandelbaum, ed., *The New Russian Foreign Policy*, pp. 100–66 (New York: Council on Foreign Relations, 1998).

38. Paul D'Anieri, Robert Kravchuk, and Taras Kuzio, *Politics and Society in Ukraine* (Boulder, Colo.: Westview, 1999); Tor Bukkvoll, *Ukraine and European Security* (London: Royal Institute of International Affairs, 1997), pp. 84–87; Anatoly S.

Gritsenko, *Civil-Military Relations in Ukraine: A System Emerging from Chaos* (Groningen, The Netherlands: Centre for European Security Studies, 1997); Andrew Wilson and Igor Burakovsky, *The Ukrainian Economy Under Kuchma* (London: Royal Institute of International Affairs, 1996), pp. 32–37.

39. Menon, "In the Shadow of the Bear"; Heinrich Tiller, "Die militärpolitische Entwicklung in den Nachfolgestaaten der ehemaligen Sowjetunion," in Hans-Hermann Höhmann, ed., *Zwischen Krise und Konsolidierung* (Munich: Carl Hanser Verlag, 1995), p. 352.

40. See Hendrik Spruyt, "The Prospects for Neoimperial and Nonimperial Outcomes in the Former Soviet Space," in Dawisha and Parrott, *End of Empire?* pp. 315–37.

41. See I. S. Koropeckyj and Gertrude Schroeder, eds., *Economics of Soviet Regions* (New York: Praeger, 1981).

42. See Motyl, "Reifying Boundaries, Fetishizing the Nation." My argument does, of course, presuppose that borders continue to be important. See John F. Helliwell, *How Much Do National Borders Matter?* (Washington, D.C.: Brookings Institution, 1998).

43. As Ekkehard W. Bornträger shows, however, border shifts are rather more commonplace than the official rhetoric concerning their inviolability would suggest. See his *Borders, Ethnicity, and National Self-Determination* (Vienna: Braumüller, 1999).

44. Olga Oliker, "An Examination of Territorial Changes Within the USSR, 1921–1980," unpublished manuscript, 1990.

45. Martha Brill Olcott, Anders Åslund, and Sherman W. Garnett, *Getting It Wrong: Regional Cooperation and the Commonwealth of Independent States* (Washington, D.C.: Carnegie Endowment for International Peace, 1999), pp. 230–32.

46. Andrea Chandler, *Institutions of Isolation: Border Controls in the Soviet Union and Its Successor States, 1917–1993* (Montreal: McGill-Queen's University Press, 1998), p. 111.

47. Paul Kolstoe, *Russians in the Former Soviet Republics* (Bloomington: Indiana University Press, 1995), pp. xi, xii, 133, 170, 244; Charles King and Neil J. Melvin, eds., *Nations Abroad: Diaspora Politics and International Relations in the Former Soviet Union* (Boulder, Colo.: Westview, 1998).

48. On Russian attitudes toward their countries of residence and their own identity, see David D. Laitin, *Identity in Formation: The Russian-Speaking Populations in the Near Abroad* (Ithaca, N.Y.: Cornell University Press, 1998); Evgenii Golovakha and Natal'ia Panina, "Rossiisko-ukrainskie otnosheniia v obshchestvennom mnenii Ukrainy i Rossii," in Dmitrii Furman, ed., *Ukraina i Rossiia: obshchestva i gosudarstva* (Moscow: Izdatel'stvo "Prava cheloveka," 1997), pp. 259–77; Richard Rose, *Russians Outside Russia: A 1991 VCIOM Survey* (Glas-

gow: Centre for the Study of Public Policy, 1997); Vera Tolz, "Conflicting 'Homeland Myths' and Nation-State Building in Postcommunist Russia," *Slavic Review* 57 (summer 1998): 267–94; Olga Alexandrova, "Russland und sein 'nahes Ausland,'" in Höhmann, *Zwischen Krise und Konsolidierung*, pp. 325, 330–33; "Vozroditsia li soiuz?" *Nezavisimaia gazeta-Stsenarii*, May 23, 1996, pp. 4–5; Motyl, "After Empire," pp. 28–30; Chauncy D. Harris, "Ethnic Tensions in Areas of the Russian Diaspora," *Post-Soviet Geography* 34 (April 1993): 233–38; Leon Aron, "The Foreign Policy Doctrine of Postcommunist Russia and Its Domestic Context," in Mandelbaum, *New Russian Foreign Policy*, pp. 23–63; Yitzhak Brudny, *Reinventing Russia: Russian Nationalism and the Soviet State, 1953–1991* (Cambridge, Mass.: Harvard University Press, 1998).

49. On the Russian economy see Richard E. Ericson, "The Post-Soviet Russian Economic System: An Industrial Feudalism?" unpublished paper, January 1999; Erik Berglöf and Romesh Vaitilingam, *Stuck in Transit: Rethinking Russian Economic Reform* (London: Centre for Economic Policy Research, 1999); Roland Götz, "Die Modernisierung Russlands: Wunsch und Wirklichkeit," *Osteuropa* 49 (July 1999): 701–17.

50. On the importance of institutions see Harry Eckstein, Frederic J. Fleron Jr., Erik P. Hoffmann, and William Reisinger, *Can Democracy Take Root in Post-Soviet Russia? Explorations in State-Society Relations* (Lanham, Md.: Rowman and Littlefield, 1998); Michael Mandelbaum, ed., *Post-Communism: Four Perspectives* (New York: Council on Foreign Relations, 1996); Stephen E. Hanson, "The Leninist Legacy and Institutional Change," *Comparative Political Studies* 28 (July 1995): 306–14; Holger Schulze, *Neo-Institutionalismus: Ein analytisches Instrumentarium zur Erklärung gesellschaftlicher Transformationsprozesse* (Berlin: Osteuropa-Institut, 1997).

51. On the possibility of Russian economic recovery, see Anders Åslund and Mikhail Dmitriev, "Economic Reform Versus Rent Seeking," in Anders Åslund and Martha Brill Olcott, eds., *Russia After Communism*, pp. 91–130 (Washington, D.C.: Carnegie Endowment for International Peace, 1999); "After the Crisis: The Russian Economy in 1999," special issue of *Harriman Review* 11 (June 1999); Clifford Gaddy and Barry Ickes, "Russia's Virtual Economy," *Foreign Affairs* 77 (September–October 1998): 53–67.

52. See Olcott, Åslund, and Garnett, *Getting It Wrong*, and Richard Sakwa and Mark Webber, "The Commonwealth of Independent States, 1991–1998: Stagnation and Survival," *Europe-Asia Studies* 51 (May 1999): 379–415, for excellent discussions of the CIS.

53. Paul D'Anieri comes to a similar conclusion in "International Cooperation Among Unequal Partners: The Emergence of Bilateralism in the Former Soviet Union," unpublished manuscript, June 1997, pp. 33–35.

54. See Miriam Lanskoy, "Caucasus," part 2 of "The NIS Observed: An Analytical Review" 5 (September 13, 2000), an electronic publication distributed by the Institute for the Study of Conflict, Ideology, and Policy at Boston University from <mlanskoy@bu.edu> on September 23, 2000.

55. On Belarus see D. E. Furman, ed., *Belorussiia i Rossiia: obshchestva i gosudarstva* (Moscow: "Prava cheloveka," 1998); Karen Dawisha and Bruce Parrott, eds., *Democratic Changes and Authoritarian Reactions in Russia, Ukraine, Belarus, and Moldova* (Cambridge: Cambridge University Press, 1997); Steven M. Eke and Taras Kuzio, "Sultanism in Eastern Europe: The Socio-Political Roots of Authoritarian Populism in Belarus," *Europe-Asia Studies* 52 (May 2000): 523–47; Uladzimir Padhol and David R. Marples, "Belarus: The Opposition and the Presidency," *Harriman Review* 12 (fall 1999): 11–18.

56. The term *Euroland* comes from *Die Zeit*.

57. These conclusions are based on numerous conversations with and presentations by policy makers, diplomats, and policy analysts from the United States and Western Europe. Unless policy experts are more prone to dissemble privately than publicly, I have no doubt that virtually no one seriously expects NATO to expand to include the Baltic states and Ukraine. See also Stephen Blank, "The Baltic States and Russia: The Strategic and Ethnic Contexts," *Harriman Review* 10 (1998): 15–32.

58. Sherman Garnett and Rachel Lebenson, "The Middle Zone and Postenlargement Europe," in Stephen J. Blank, ed., *NATO After Enlargement: New Challenges, New Missions, New Forces*, pp. 73–93 (Carlisle, Penn.: Strategic Studies Institute, 1998); F. Stephen Larrabee, "Ukraine's Place in European and Regional Security," in Lubomyr A. Hajda, ed., *Ukraine in the World* (Cambridge, Mass.: Ukrainian Research Institute, 1998), p. 261. See Paul D'Anieri and Bruan Schmiedeler, "European Security After the Cold War: The Policy of 'Insulationism,'" paper presented at the Midwest Conference of the International Studies Association, East Lansing, Mich., November 21, 1992; Vladimir Baranovsky, ed., *Russia and Europe: The Emerging Security Agenda* (Oxford: Oxford University Press, 1997).

59. Timothy Garton Ash, "Europe's Endangered Liberal Order," *Foreign Affairs* 77 (March–April 1998): 51–65; "Survey: EMU," *Economist*, April 11, 1998, pp. 1–22; Sergey Rogov, *Russia and NATO's Enlargement* (Alexandria, Va.: Center for Naval Analyses, 1995); Michael Mandelbaum, *NATO Expansion: A Bridge to the Nineteenth Century* (Chevy Chase, Md.: Center for Political and Strategic Studies, 1997).

60. See Madeleine Albright, "Enlarging NATO," *Economist*, February 15, 1997, pp. 21–23; James Sher, *Ukraine's New Time of Troubles* (Camberley, U.K.: Conflict Studies Research Centre, 1998); Bruce Clark, "NATO," *Economist*, April 24, 1999, pp. 3–18.

61. Eric van Breska, Martin Brusis, Claus Gierig, Andras Inotai, and Monika Wohlfeld, eds., *Costs, Benefits, and Chances of Eastern Enlargement for the European Union* (Gütersloh, Germany: Bertelsmann Foundation, 1998); John Peet, "European Union," *Economist*, May 31, 1997, pp. 13–15. On antidumping actions see World Bank, *Entering the Twenty-first Century: World Development Report, 1999–2000* (New York: Oxford University Press, 2000), pp. 56–60.

62. European Union, *Agenda 2000: Eine stärkere und erweiterte Union* (Brussels: Europäische Kommission, 1997); Advisory Council on International Affairs, *An Inclusive Europe* (The Hague: Advisory Council on International Affairs, 1997).

63. Center for Peace, Conversion, and Foreign Policy of Ukraine, "Ukraine on the Way to the European Union," occasional report no. 71, Kyiv, October 15, 1998; Werner Weidenfeld, ed., *Central and Eastern Europe on the Way to the European Union* (Gütersloh, Germany: Bertelsmann Foundation, 1995); Robert Cottrell, "Europe Survey," *Economist*, October 23, 1999, pp. 14–15; Clark, "NATO."

64. Among other things, membership in the EU would, according to existing EU regulations, require that Estonia, Slovenia, Poland, Hungary, and the Czech Republic abandon their free-trade agreements with their eastern neighbors. See Breffni O'Rourke, "Eastern Europe: EU, Eastern Candidates Discuss Sensitive Trade Issues," <http://www.rferl.org/nca/features/1999/05/F.RU.990520134805.html> (June 7, 1999).

65. See Rey Koslowski, "European Migration Regimes: Emerging, Enlarging, and Deteriorating," *Journal of Ethnic and Migration Studies* 24 (October 1998): 735–49; Olcott, Åslund, and Garnett, *Getting It Wrong*, pp. 198–99.

66. Oleksandr Pavliuk, *The European Union and Ukraine: The Need for a New Vision* (New York: EastWest Institute, 1999).

67. Michael Ludwig, "Angst vor einer neuen Mauer im Osten Polens," *Frankfurter Allgemeine Zeitung*, July 5, 2000, p. 6; Natalia Tchourikova, "Ukraine: EU Entry Depends on Internal Developments," *RFE/RL Weekday Magazine*, October 21, 1998; Reuters, "Kuchma Says European Union Slights Ukraine," October 28, 1998, electronically distributed by *Ukraine List*, no. 88, September 12, 2000, ed. Dominique Arel, Brown University <darel@brown.edu>.

68. Center for Peace, Conversion, and Foreign Policy of Ukraine, *Foreign Policy of Ukraine Newsletter*, March 11–17, 2000, p. 10. Slovakia followed in the footsteps of the Czech Republic, which imposed a new visa regime in early 2000. See Center for Peace, Conversion, and Foreign Policy of Ukraine, *Foreign Policy of Ukraine Newsletter*, January 8–14, 2000, p. 4.

69. Helmut Schmidt, "Wer nicht zu Europa gehört," *Die Zeit* <http://www.zeit.de/2000/41/Politik/200041_selbstbehauptung.html> (October 11, 2000); "Survey: European Union," *Economist*, May 31, 1997, p. 14.

70. On globalization see Richard Langhorne, *The Coming of Globalization* (London: St. Martin's, 2001); Ulrich Beck, *Was Ist Globalisierung?* (Frankfurt am Main: Suhrkamp, 1997); *Is Global Capitalism Working? A Foreign Affairs Reader* (New York: Council on Foreign Relations, 1999).

71. See Edward Luttwak, *Turbo-Capitalism: Winners and Losers in the Global Economy* (New York: HarperCollins, 1999).

72. Alexander Gerschenkron, *Economic Backwardness in Historical Perspective* (New York: Praeger, 1962).

73. Heinz Timmermann, "Russland: Strategischer Partner der Europäischen Union? Interessen, Impulse, Widersprüche," *Osteuropa* 49 (October 1999): 1003.

74. Otto Kirchheimer, "Confining Conditions and Revolutionary Breakthroughs," *American Political Science Review* 4 (December 1965): 964–74. Of course, it is also perfectly possible for revolutionaries to preach market reform. See Motyl, *Revolutions, Nations, Empires*, pp. 32–36.

75. Olcott, Åslund, and Garnett, *Getting It Wrong*, pp. 69–72.

76. Motyl, *Revolutions, Nations, Empires*, pp. 43–50.

77. For a similar argument see Georgi M. Derlugian, "Rouge et Noire: Contradictions of the Soviet Collapse," *Telos* 26 (summer 1993): 13–25.

78. Johan Galtung, "Geopolitics After the Cold War: An Essay in Agenda Theory," in Armand Clesse, Richard Cooper, and Yoshikazu Sakamoto, eds., *The International System After the Collapse of the East-West Order* (Dordrecht, The Netherlands: Martinus Nijhoff, 1994), p. 202.

79. Motyl, *Revolutions, Nations, Empires*, pp. 157–61.

Conclusion: Losing Empire

1. Karen Dawisha, "Constructing and Deconstructing Empire in the Post-Soviet Space," in Karen Dawisha and Bruce Parrott, eds., *The End of Empire? The Transformation of the USSR in Comparative Perspective* (Armonk, N. Y.: Sharpe, 1997), p. 342.

2. See Mark Beissinger and Crawford Young, eds., *The Search for the Efficacious State in Africa and Eurasia* (forthcoming); Valerie Sperling, "The Domestic and International Obstacles to State-Building in Russia," in Valerie Sperling, ed., *Building the Russian State: Institutional Crisis and the Quest for Democratic Governance*, pp. 1–23 (Boulder, Colo.: Westview, 2000); Allen Lynch, "The Crisis of the State in Russia," *International Spectator* 30 (April–June 1995): 21–33.

3. Leslie Dienes, "Corporate Russia: Privatization and Prospects in the Oil and Gas Sector," Donald W. Treadgold Papers in Russian, East European, and

Central Asian Studies, no. 5, March 1996, Henry M. Jackson School of International Studies, University of Washington, Seattle.

4. See Thomas Graham, "A World Without Russia?" paper presented at the Jamestown Foundation, Washington, D.C., on June 9, 1999.

5. Gerhard Simon, "Die Disintegration der Sowjetunion," in Alexander Demandt, ed., *Das Ende der Weltreiche: Von den Persen bis zur Sowjetunion* (Munich: Beck, 1997), pp. 209–10.

6. John Peet, "European Union," *Economist*, May 31, 1997, pp. 13–15.

7. See Helmut Schmidt, "Wege aus Europas Krise," *Die Zeit*, October 14, 1999, pp. 6–7; Andrew Moravcsik, ed., *Centralization or Fragmentation? Europe Facing the Challenges of Deepening, Diversity, and Democracy* (New York: Council on Foreign Relations, 1998). For an especially alarmist view see Martin Feldstein, "EMU and International Conflict," *Foreign Affairs* 76 (November–December 1997): 60–73.

8. Joseph S. Nye Jr., "Redefining the National Interest," *Foreign Affairs* 78 (July–August 1999): 22–35; Peter W. Rodman, "The Fallout from Kosovo," *Foreign Affairs* 78 (July–August 1999): 45–51.

Index